HOW TO MEDITATE

A Practical Guide

How to Meditate

A Practical Guide

Kathleen McDonald

Edited by Robina Courtin

WISDOM PUBLICATIONS

WISDOM PUBLICATIONS
199 Elm Street
Somerville, Massachusetts 02144 USA

Library of Congress Cataloging-in-Publication Data

McDonald Kathleen, 1952–

How to meditate : a practical guide / Kathleen McDonald ; edited by Robina Courtin.

p.   cm.

Includes bibliographical references.

ISBN 0-86171-009-6

1. Meditation. 2. Devotional exercises. I. Courtin, Robina. II. Title.

BL627.M36   1984

294.3'443—dc20   88–51646

ISBN 0 86171 009 6

04   03   02
17   16   15   14

Cover: detail from a thangka of Maphampa, one of the famous Sixteen Arhants, by an unknown eighteenth-century Tibetan artist. Courtesy of Tibet House, New Delhi.

Wisdom Publications' books are printed on acid-free paper and meet the guidelines for permanence and durability of the Committee on Production Guidelines for Book Longevity of the Council on Library Resources.

Printed in Canada

Contents

Preface

This book has come about because of an ever-increasing interest in meditation and a shortage of practical information on how to do it. It is written primarily for those who want to start practising, but should also be of interest to anyone who simply wants to know what meditation is all about.

There are hundreds of meditation methods taught by the various spiritual traditions, and choosing the right practices, the right path, is a matter of personal investigation and experience. Most of the techniques here come from the Mahayana Buddhist tradition of Tibet, several from the Theravada tradition of South East Asia, and a few are my own improvisations on Buddhist themes.

I have tried to explain them simply and clearly, without any technical language, because I want to show that Buddhism is practical and down-to-earth, not a dry philosophy or an exotic cult. Throughout, the emphasis is on *experience*, using meditation to actually bring about changes in our thoughts, feelings and actions.

Part One, *Mind and Meditation*, lays the foundation, explaining why people meditate and how they benefit from it. Part Two, *Establishing a Meditation Practice,* gives basic information and advice for beginning practitioners. In the rest of the book I present the actual meditation methods. I have divided them into four parts, *Meditations on the Mind, Analytical Meditations, Visualization Meditations* and *Devotional Practices.* Each technique has a preamble that gives some background to the meditation, shows its benefits and how best to do it, and explains its practical application. Finally, there are the phonetics in Tibetan of the prayers in Part Six, a glossary of terms and a list of titles for suggested further reading.

ACKNOWLEDGEMENTS

Anything I might know about meditation is due chiefly to the contact I have had with Lama Thubten Yeshe (1935–1984) and Lama Thubten Zopa Rinpoche, two Tibetan Buddhist masters who have devoted their time and energy during the last fifteen years to instructing and guiding Westerners interested in Buddhist philosophy and meditation. As a result of their efforts the Foundation for the Preservation of the Mahayana Tradition (FPMT), established by them in 1975, has grown to include over thirty meditation centres throughout the world where people live, study and meditate.

I thank Lama Yeshe and Lama Zopa from my heart for sharing with us their knowledge and insight and pray sincerely that their work may continue for a long time to come.

Many of the meditation practices here have been adapted from the teachings of Lama Yeshe and Lama Zopa, but I am also grateful to Geshe Ngawang Dhargyey, Geshe Jampa Tekchok and Sogyal Rinpoche who have also been my sources.

Many people have worked to make this book possible. I extend thanks to Wendy Finster for her *Handbook of Mahayana Practices,* from which this book developed; to Thubten Angmo, Jon Landaw and T. Yeshe for their initial editing and translating work; to Nick Ribush, Yeshe Khadro, Thubten Pende, Steve Carlier, Lorraine Rees, Peter Rees, James Payne, Tim Young, Jan Courtin, Marshall Harris, Sarah Thresher,

Karin Zeitvogel, and the nuns of Dorje Pamo Monastery for their invaluable suggestions; and finally to my editor Robina Courtin who has worked with me throughout to rewrite and reshape *How to Meditate* in an effort to make it as clear and practical as possible.

Kathleen McDonald
(Sangye Khadro)
Dorje Pamo Monastery
Lavaur, France
June, 1984

For my parents
Who have helped me so much.
May they discover the highest peace
within themselves.

Part One
Mind and
Meditation

1 *Why Meditate?*

Everyone wants happiness yet few of us seem to find it. In our search for satisfaction we go from one relationship to another, one job to another, one country to another. We study art and medicine, train to be tennis players and typists; have babies, race cars, write books and grow flowers. We spend our money on elaborate stereo systems, home computers, comfortable furniture and vacations in the sun. Or we try to get back to nature, eat whole-food, practise yoga and meditate. Just about everything we do is an attempt to find real happiness and avoid suffering.

There is nothing wrong with any of these things; there is nothing wrong with having relationships and possessions. The problem is that we see them as having some inherent ability to satisfy us, as being the *cause* of happiness. But they cannot be – simply because they do not last. Everything by nature constantly changes and eventually disappears: our body, our friends, all our belongings, the environment. Our dependence on impermanent things and clinging to the rainbow-like happiness they bring cause only disappointment and grief, not satisfaction and contentment.

We *do* experience happiness with things outside ourselves,

but it doesn't truly satisfy us or free us from our problems. It is poor-quality happiness, unreliable and short-lived. This does not mean that we should give up our friends and possessions in order to be happy. Rather, what we need to give up are our misconceptions about them and our unrealistic expectations of what they can do for us.

Not only do we see them as permanent and able to satisfy us; at the root of our problems is our fundamentally mistaken view of reality (see page 58). We believe instinctively that people and things exist in and of themselves, from their own side; that they have an inherent nature, an inherent thingness. This means that we see things as having certain qualities abiding naturally within them; that they are, from their own side, good or bad, attractive or unattractive. These qualities seem to be out there, in the objects themselves, quite independent of our viewpoint and everything else.

We think, for example, that chocolate is inherently delicious or that success is inherently satisfying. But surely, if they were, they would never fail to give pleasure or to satisfy, and everyone would experience them in the same way.

Our mistaken idea is deeply-ingrained and habitual; it colours all our relationships and dealings with the world. We probably rarely question whether or not the way we see things is the way they actually exist, but once we do it will be obvious that our picture of reality is exaggerated and one-sided; that the good and bad qualities we see in things are actually created and projected by our own mind.

According to Buddhism there *is* lasting, stable happiness and everyone has the potential to experience it. The causes of happiness lie within our own mind, and methods for achieving it can be practised by anyone, anywhere, in any lifestyle – living in the city, working an eight-hour job, raising a family, playing at weekends.

By practising these methods – meditation – we can learn to be happy at any time, in any situation, even difficult and painful ones. Eventually we can free ourselves of problems like dissatisfaction, anger and anxiety and, finally, by realizing the actual way that things exist, we will eliminate completely the very source of all disturbing states of mind so that they will never arise again.

What is the mind?

Mind, or consciousness, is at the heart of Buddhist theory and practice, and for the last two-and-a-half thousand years meditators have been investigating and using it as a means of transcending unsatisfactory existence and achieving perfect peace. It is said that all happiness, ordinary and sublime, is achieved by understanding and transforming our own mind.

A non-physical kind of energy, the mind's function is to know, to experience. It is awareness itself. It is clear in nature and reflects everything that it experiences, just as a still lake reflects the surrounding mountains and forests.

Mind changes from moment to moment. It is a beginningless continuum, like an ever-flowing stream: the previous mind-moment gave rise to this mind-moment, which gives rise to the next mind-moment, and so on. It is the general name given to the totality of our conscious and unconscious experiences: each of us is the centre of a world of thoughts, perceptions, feelings, memories and dreams – all of these are mind.

Mind is not a physical thing that *has* thoughts and feelings; it *is* those very experiences. Being non-matter, it is different from the body, although mind and body are interconnected and interdependent. Mind, consciousness, is carried through our body by subtle physical energies (see page 134), which also control our movement and vital functions. This relationship explains why, for example, physical sickness and discomfort can affect our state of mind and why, in turn, mental attitudes can both give rise to and heal physical problems.

Mind can be compared to an ocean, and momentary mental events such as happiness, irritation, fantasies and boredom to the waves that rise and fall on its surface. Just as the waves can subside to reveal the stillness of the ocean's depths, so too is it possible to calm the turbulence of our mind to reveal its natural pristine clarity.

The ability to do this lies within the mind itself and the key to the mind is meditation.

2 What is Meditation?

Subduing the mind and bringing it to the right understanding of reality is no easy task. It requires a slow and gradual process of *listening* to and reading explanations on the mind and the nature of things; *thinking* about and carefully analyzing this information; and finally transforming the mind through *meditation*.

The mind can be divided into *sense consciousness* – sight, hearing, smell, taste and touch – and *mental consciousness*. Mental consciousness ranges from our grossest experiences of anger or desire, for example, to the subtlest level of complete stillness and clarity. It includes our intellectual processes, our feelings and emotions, our memory and our dreams.

Meditation is an activity of the mental consciousness. It involves one part of the mind observing, analyzing and dealing with the rest of the mind. Meditation can take many forms: concentrating single-pointedly on an (internal) object, trying to understand some personal problem, generating a joyful love for all humanity, praying to an object of devotion, or communicating with our own inner wisdom. Its ultimate aim is to awaken a very subtle level of consciousness and to use it to discover reality, directly and intuitively.

This direct, intuitive awareness of how things are is known as enlightenment and is the end result of Mahayana Buddhist practice. The purpose of reaching it – and the driving force behind all practice – is to help others reach it too.

The Tibetan term for meditation *(sgom)* means, literally, "to become familiar." There are many different meditation techniques and many things in the mind to become familiar with. Each technique has specific functions and benefits and each is a part of the framework for bringing our mind to a realistic view of the world.

It might be best to start by saying what meditation is *not*, because there are many misunderstandings about it. For one thing, meditation is not simply a matter of sitting in a particular posture or breathing a particular way; it is a state of mind. Although the best results usually come when we meditate in a quiet place, we can also meditate while working, walking, riding on a bus or cooking dinner. One Tibetan meditator realized emptiness (see page 58) while chopping wood and another attained single-pointed concentration while cleaning his teacher's room.

First, we learn to develop the meditative state of mind in formal, sitting practice, but once we are good at it we can be more freestyle and creative and can generate this mental state at any time, in any situation. By then, meditation has become a way of life.

Meditation is not something foreign or unsuitable for the Western mind. There are different methods practised in different cultures, but they all share the common principle of the mind simply becoming familiar with various aspects of itself. And the mind of every person, Eastern or Western, has the same basic elements and experiences, the same basic problem – and the same potential.

Meditation is not spacing-out or running away. In fact, it is being totally honest with ourselves: taking a good look at what we are and working with that in order to become more positive and useful, to ourselves and others. There are both positive and negative aspects of the mind. The negative aspects – our mental disorders or, quite literally, delusions – include jealousy, anger, desire, pride and the like. These arise from our misunderstanding of reality and habitual clinging to the way we see things. Through meditation we can recognize our mistakes and adjust our mind to think and react more realistically, more honestly.

The final goal, enlightenment, is a long-term one. But meditations done with this goal in mind can and do have enormous short-term benefits. As our concrete picture of reality softens we develop a more positive and realistic self-image and are thus more relaxed and less anxious. We learn to have fewer unrealistic expectations of the people and things around us and therefore meet with less disappointment; relationships improve and life becomes more stable and satisfying.

But remember, lifelong habits die hard. It is difficult enough simply to recognize our anger and jealousy, much less make an effort to hold back the old familiar tide of feeling or analyze its causes and results. Transforming the mind is a slow and gradual process. It is a matter of ridding ourselves, bit by bit, of instinctive, harmful habit patterns and "becoming familiar" with habits that necessarily bring positive results – to ourselves and others.

There are many meditation techniques but all can be included under two headings: *stabilizing* and *analytical*.

Stabilizing meditation

In general, this type of meditation is used to develop what is known as single-pointed concentration – a prerequisite for any lasting insight. The aim is to concentrate upon one object – the breath, the nature of one's own mind, a concept, a visualized image – without interruption.

Concentration without interruption is the exact opposite of our usual state of mind. If you turn inwards for a few moments you will notice your mind jumping from one thing to another: a thought of something you will do later, a sound outside, a friend, something that happened earlier, a physical sensation, a cup of coffee. We never need to say to the mind, "Think!" or "Feel!" It is always busy doing something, speeding along, an energy of its own.

With such a scattered and uncontrolled mind there is little chance of success in anything we do, whether it is remembering a telephone number, cooking a meal or running a business. And certainly, without concentration successful meditation is impossible.

Stabilizing meditation is not easy, but it is essential for bringing the mind under control. Although the development of actual single-pointed concentration is the work of full-time meditators, we don't need to retreat to the mountains to experience the benefits of this kind of meditation: even in our day-to-day city life we can develop good concentration by regularly doing ten or fifteen minutes a day of stabilizing meditation – keeping the mind focused on a single object and letting go of all other thoughts. It brings an immediate sense of spaciousness and allows us to see the workings of our mind more clearly, both during the meditation and throughout the rest of the day.

Analytical meditation

This type of meditation brings into play creative, intellectual thought and is crucial to our development: the first step in gaining any real insight is to understand *conceptually* how things are. This conceptual clarity develops into firm conviction which, when combined with stabilizing meditation, brings direct and intuitive knowing.

However, even before we can "know how things are" we must first identify our *wrong* conceptions. Using clear, penetrative, analytical thought we unravel the complexities of our attitudes and behaviour patterns. Gradually, we can eliminate those thoughts, feelings and ideas that cause ourselves and others unhappiness, and in their place cultivate thoughts, feelings and ideas that bring happiness.

In this way we become familiar with the reality of, for example, cause and effect – that our present experiences are the result of our past actions *and* the cause of our future experiences – or with the fact that all things lack an inherent nature. We can meditate point by point on the benefits of patience and the disadvantages of anger; on the value of developing compassion; on the kindness of others.

In one sense, an analytical meditation session is an intensive study session. However, the level of conceptual thought that we can reach during these meditations is more subtle and therefore more potent than our thoughts during day-to-day life. Because our senses are not being bombarded by the usual frantic input we are able to concentrate more strongly and develop a finely-tuned sensitivity to the workings of our mind.

Stabilizing and analytical meditations are complementary and are often used together in one session. When doing a meditation on emptiness (page 58), for example, we analyze the object (emptiness) using information we have heard or read, as well as our own thoughts, feelings and memories. At some point an intuitive experience of or conviction about the object arises. We should then stop thinking and focus our attention single-pointedly on the feeling for as long as possible. We should soak our mind in the experience. When the feeling fades we can either continue analyzing or conclude the session.

This method of combining the two kinds of meditation causes the mind literally to become one with the object of meditation. The stronger our concentration, the deeper our insight will be. We need to repeat this process again and again with anything we want to understand in order to transform our insight into actual experience.

Stabilizing meditations such as the breathing meditations

(page 44) will also go better if some skilful analysis is used. When we sit down to meditate we should start by examining our state of mind and clarifying our motivation for doing the practice, and this involves analytical thought. During the meditation itself we might find concentration especially diffi-cult; at such times it is good to analyze the problem for a few moments, then to re-place the mind on the breath. And sometimes it is useful to check on the mind during the meditation to make sure it is not day-dreaming but doing what it is supposed to be doing.

The meditations in this book are divided into four sections. The first of these, *Meditations on the Mind,* includes three techniques that help develop awareness of the mind itself. The breathing meditation (often called mindfulness medita-tion) is primarily a stabilizing practice that uses the breath as the object of concentration. Beginners are advised to start with this practice as it calms the mind, enabling us to see more clearly how it works.

The other meditations in this section are for developing an awareness of the clear nature of the mind, and the begin-ninglessness and continuity of the mind. All techniques involve both stabilization and analysis.

The next section, *Analytical Meditations,* offers seven techniques for looking into and analyzing our assumptions about how things exist, about life, death, suffering and com-passion; and, finally, advice on dealing with our negative energy in everyday life. If you are just learning to slow the mind down with, say, the breathing meditation, you might not feel ready to tackle any of these subjects in formal medi-tation; however, simply reading through this section pro-vides plenty of food for thought.

Next is *Visualization Meditations*: six techniques introduce visualization as used in Vajrayana practice; all combine stabi-lization and analysis.

The final section of the main body of the book, *Devotional*

Practices, includes several more meditations as well as prayers and other practices.

It is important to go slowly and to adopt new methods only when you are ready. There is no point in trying to do meditations that seem strange or complicated or whose purpose is not clear. It is better to stick to one or two methods whose benefits you can really experience.

However, everything in this book is an integral part of balanced spiritual growth and a step on a path that is vast and profound. Through careful and patient study and practice you will learn to appreciate the relationship that these practices have to each other and to the entire path.

Part Two
Establishing
a Meditation
Practice

1 *Advice for Beginners*

Regular practice

In order to experience the benefits of meditation it is necessary to practise regularly; as with any activity, it is not
possible to succeed unless we dedicate our energy whole-
heartedly to it. Try to meditate every day, or at least several
times a week. If you let weeks or months pass without
meditating you will get out of shape and find it all the more
difficult when you try again. Inevitably there will be times
when the last thing you want to do is meditate, but meditate
anyway, even for only a few minutes; often these sessions are
the most productive.

The meditation place

It is best to reserve a room or corner especially for your
meditation sessions.

Set up your seat, either a cushion on the floor, on a bed or
sofa, or a straight-backed chair, with a table or low bench in
front of you for this and other books that you need for your
meditations.

Make the place as comfortable and as pleasing to your
senses as possible. It should be quiet and clean, a place you are

glad to be in and ideally where you cannot easily be disturbed.

If you are so inclined you can set up an altar nearby for pictures that inspire you, for example, or for candles, incense or other offerings. The point is, you should surround yourself with things that are conducive to good meditation, such that you can't wait to return!

Choosing a practice

It is good to start with one of the breathing meditations on page 44. These are ideal for calming the mind and starting to develop some insight into your thoughts and feelings – and both calm and insight are essential ingredients for successful meditations of any kind.

Once you are familiar with meditating you should choose the practices that best suit your temperament and natural inclinations, remembering that each technique is an antidote to a particular problem. If, for example, you are inclined towards anger you should meditate on patience and loving kindness (pages 94 and 121). If you are disturbed by strong desire and attachment you can meditate on impermanence (page 77), death (page 68) or suffering (page 81). If you are depressed you can meditate on the preciousness and potential of your human life (page 63).

If, however, your mind is tranquil you can practise the development of concentration with, for example, a visualization technique that appeals to you (page 109), or deepen your insight into the nature of reality by meditating on emptiness (page 58).

If you appreciate the benefits of devotional practices, you can incorporate prostrations and prayers (page 144) into your practice.

All this is meant as a general guide only; with practice you will learn to know what to do when. However, the importance of being guided by an experienced meditator cannot be over-emphasized (see below).

Short sessions

In the beginning it is best to meditate for short periods – ten to thirty minutes – and end your session while mind and body are still comfortable and fresh. If you push yourself to meditate too long and rise from your seat with an aching body and a frustrated mind, you won't have much interest in sitting down to meditate again. Meditation should be a satisfying and productive experience, not a burden.

You should decide beforehand on a period of time for the session and stick to it, even if the meditation is going well. As your skill develops you can increase the length of your sessions accordingly.

Be relaxed but alert

Mind and body should be relaxed and comfortable throughout the session. You can relax mentally by firmly deciding to leave behind all problems, worries and involvements of the external world and immerse yourself in the silence of your inner world. It might help to recall a past experience of feeling at ease and contented – and then generate that same feeling on your meditation seat.

Breathing meditation can also bring the same result. Observing the gentle, natural rhythm of the breath and avoiding distracting thoughts, your mental state gradually becomes tranquil and clear. But don't fall asleep! Stay alert. Take note of whatever thoughts, images, feelings and sensations arise in your mind without becoming involved in them. Your main focus of attention should always be the breath (or whatever subject you have chosen to meditate on).

Physical relaxation can be facilitated by the practice of such disciplines as hatha yoga, tai chi, kum nye or other stress-reduction and relaxation methods. Literature and courses on these techniques are available in most cities. Any means you use to ease physical tension and improve your ability to sit in meditation is a valuable addition to your practice.

No expectations

Since we all want to enjoy happiness and peace of mind and avoid problems, it is natural to want good experiences during meditation. But such expectations are not necessarily realistic and are likely to hinder your progress. The mind is complex and ever-changing. One day you might have a calm, joyful meditation and the next a meditation beset by distractions and turmoil. This is quite normal and should not cause worry or frustration. Be ready for anything and do not be disturbed by whatever happens. The most troublesome painful experiences can be the most valuable in terms of the growth of wisdom.

Feel satisfied that you are making the effort to meditate and transform your mind – that itself *is* meditation. As long as you are trying it is mistaken to think that you can't meditate. Results take time. Don't be discouraged if you have not achieved good concentration within a few weeks; it is better to think in terms of years. Habits built up over a lifetime are not eliminated instantly but by gradual cultivation of new habits. So, be easy on yourself. Recognize your capabilities and limitations and evaluate your progress accordingly.

The need for a teacher

The most effective way to learn anything is to study with someone who has already mastered it – and meditation is no exception. The mind can be compared to a musical instrument: in order to create beautiful music with it we need to study with a master who knows the instrument inside and out, and in order to develop a clear, enthusiastic and loving mind we need the guidance of someone who thoroughly understands how the mind works and how it can be transformed.

However, it is not easy to find a qualified teacher. The qualities to look for include compassion, knowledge and insight, morality, sincerity and skill in explanation. You should have confidence in your teacher and communicate well with him or her. Therefore, it might be a matter of years before you meet the right teacher. But don't think you should set out on a frantic guru hunt! Take it easy. When the time is right you will meet the person who can guide you successfully.

In the meantime, you can practise meditations such as those explained here, and seek the advice of any practitioner whose qualities you admire – even if the person has been meditating for only a short time. Your own innate wisdom, your inner guru, will tell you whether or not you are heading in the right direction.

Don't advertise!

Whenever we discover something new and interesting we feel like telling everyone about it, but it is not a good idea to talk too much about your meditation. Unless someone is sincerely interested and asks you about it, it is better to keep quiet. Broadcasting your experiences will dissipate whatever good energy and insight you have gained. It is best to discuss your practice only with your teacher and a few close friends.

Having taken up meditation there is no need to make big changes in your lifestyle, behaviour or appearance. You can keep your job and your friends, continue to live in your nice house and just enjoy life as usual.

Meditation is an internal, not external, activity. Your practice will transform your mind on a subtle level, making you more sensitive and clear, and giving you fresh insight into ordinary day-to-day experiences. Superficial changes are not natural and are unlikely to impress anyone, but the deep, natural changes created by meditation are real and beneficial, both for yourself and others.

2 The Meditation Session

Sit

Sit comfortably in either the seven-point posture or some other recommended position (see page 34). Spend a few minutes settling your body and mind. Decide which meditation you will do and for how long you will meditate, and determine not to do anything else for that period of time.

It is traditional to prostrate three times before sitting down to meditate (see page 150). Prostration counteracts pride. It expresses our acceptance that we have work to do, problems to solve, and a long way to go in our inner development. It is not necessarily an act of submission to something external, but a recognition that the potential for wholeness and perfection lies within us. We are prostrating to our own true nature, which we want to awaken through meditation. If done with this understanding, prostration helps put the mind in the right state for meditation.

Motivate

Check up on your thoughts. Why do you want to meditate? What do you hope to achieve? As with any activity, the clearer and more firmly we set our goal, the stronger is our motivation and the more likely we are to succeed.

A short-term goal of meditation is simply to calm down and relax. More far-reaching is the aim eventually to penetrate through to a complete understanding of the nature of reality as an antidote to unhappiness and dissatisfaction. However, the most altruistic and thus the highest aim of meditation is to achieve enlightenment in order to help others gain it, too. This is the most far-reaching objective – the Mahayana motivation – and inevitably the other goals will be reached on the way.

Whichever your motivation, think it through clearly before proceeding with your meditation.

If you feel it would help your practice you can say either all the preliminary prayers on page 144 or just the prayer of refuge and bodhicitta. Some people find that reciting prayers, either mentally or verbally, induces a good frame of mind for meditation by reminding them of the wisdom and other qualities they want to achieve. If you do pray, reflect on the meaning of each prayer so that it flows naturally from your heart.

Meditate

Now, turn to the object of meditation and keep it firmly in mind throughout the period. Follow the advice on page 37 if you come up against problems during the session.

If you do a stabilizing meditation – for example, focusing on the breath – aim to hold your mind unwaveringly on the object of concentration.

If you do an analytical meditation, investigate the topic with full attention until an intuitive feeling of it arises, then place your mind single-pointedly – in other words, do stabilizing meditation – on that insight so that it becomes literally one with your experience. When the feeling or your concentration start to fade, return to the analytical process.

Before starting the meditation it is important to read the preamble and then to integrate into the meditation – especially analytical meditation – the ideas raised there.

End the meditation with a firm conclusion about the topic, based on your insight and experiences during the session.

Ideally, of course, it be would best not to need to refer to this or other books during your meditation, but until you know the details you cannot avoid having to open your eyes from time to time to check on the next stage of the meditation. Experiment to find the most comfortable way to conduct your sessions.

It is very useful to follow the meditations on a cassette tape, or to take it in turns with a fellow meditator to read out the meditations to each other.

Whichever method you use, the important point is to be relaxed and rid of all unrealistic expectations about the way you think the session should go. Follow the instructions, and your own wisdom, as well as you can, don't panic and have confidence!

Dedicate

Each time you meditate, even for just a few minutes, you create positive energy and develop some degree of insight. The effects of this energy and insight are determined by your thoughts and attitudes as you move from meditation to ordinary activity. If you finish the session in an unhappy frame of mind or rush off too quickly, much of the energy is likely to be lost.

Before you leave your meditation seat, take a few minutes to recall your reasons and motivation for doing the session and dedicate your energy and insight to the fulfilment of these objectives. Clear dedication in this way stabilizes the insight and ensures that results come.

And don't forget to bring the good experiences of the meditation into your daily activities. Instead of acting and reacting impulsively and following your thoughts and feelings here and there, watch your mind carefully, be aware, and try to deal skilfully with problems as they arise. If you can do this each day, your meditation has been successful.

3   Posture

Mind and body are interdependent. Because the state of one affects the state of the other, a correct sitting posture is emphasized for meditation. The seven-point posture, used by experienced meditators for centuries, is recommended as the best way to help gain a calm, clear state of mind.

1 Legs

If possible, sit with your legs crossed in the vajra, or full-lotus, position where each foot is placed, sole upward, on the thigh of the opposite leg. This position is difficult to maintain but by practising each day you will find that your body slowly adapts and you are able to sit this way for increasingly longer periods. The vajra posture gives the best support to the body, but is not essential.

An alternative position is the half-lotus where the left foot is on the floor under the right leg and the right foot on top of the left thigh. You can also sit in a simple cross-legged posture with both feet on the floor.

A firm cushion under the buttocks will enable you to keep your back straight and sit longer without getting pins-and-needles in your legs and feet.

If you are unable to sit on the floor in any of these positions, you can meditate in a chair or on a low, slanted bench. The important thing is to be comfortable.

2 *Arms*

Hold your hands loosely on your lap, about two inches below the navel, right hand on top of the left, palms upward, with the fingers aligned. The two hands should be slightly cupped so that the tips of the thumbs meet to form a triangle. Shoulders and arms should be relaxed. Your arms should not be pressed against your body but held a few inches away to allow circulation of air: this helps to prevent sleepiness.

3 *Back*

Your back is most important. It should be straight, held relaxed and lightly upright, as if the vertebrae were a pile of coins. It might be difficult in the beginning, but in time it will become natural and you will notice the benefits: your energy will flow more freely (see page 134), you won't feel sluggish, and you will be able to sit comfortably in meditation for increasingly longer periods.

4 *Eyes*

New meditators often find it easier to concentrate with their eyes fully closed. This is quite acceptable. However, it is recommended that you leave your eyes slightly open to admit a little light, and direct your gaze downwards. Closing your eyes may be an invitation to sluggishness, sleep or dream-like images, all of which hinder meditation.

5 *Jaw*

Your jaw should be relaxed and teeth slightly apart, not clenched. Your mouth should also be relaxed, with the lips together lightly.

6 *Tongue*

The tip of your tongue should touch the palate just behind the upper teeth. This reduces the flow of saliva and thus the need to swallow, both of which are hindrances as your concentration increases and you sit in meditation for longer periods.

7 *Head*

Your neck should be bent forward a little so that your gaze is directed naturally towards the floor in front of you. If your head is held too high you may have problems with mental wandering and agitation, and if dropped too low you could experience mental heaviness or sleepiness.

This seven-point posture is most conducive to clear, unobstructed contemplation. You might find it difficult in the beginning, but it is a good idea to go through each point at the start of your session and try to maintain the correct posture for a few minutes. With familiarity it will feel more natural and you will begin to notice its benefits.

The practice of hatha yoga or other physical disciplines can be a great help in loosening tight muscles and joints, thus enabling you to sit more comfortably. However, if you are unable to adapt to sitting cross-legged you can make a compromise between perfect posture and a relaxed state. In other words, keep your body and mind happy, comfortable and free of tension.

4 Common Problems

Mental excitement

At times during a meditation session the mind is very restless and our attention is continually distracted by other things. This tends to happen when we're feeling excited and happy. Our thoughts turn to people we love, good experiences we've had, conversations, places and films we've enjoyed. Normally we just let the mind run like this without trying to control it, so mental wandering has become a deeply in-grained habit.

It is not easy to give up habits, but we should recognize that this one is the very opposite of meditation. As long as we are busy running in circles on the surface of the mind we will never penetrate to its depths and never develop the concentration we need for perceiving reality.

There are a number of methods for counteracting mental excitement. One is to focus firmly on the breath and let the mind become as calm and even as the natural rhythm of your breathing (see page 44). Each time your attention wanders, bring it back to the breath. Observe whatever thoughts and feelings arise without getting involved in them; recall that they are just waves of your mind, rising and falling. Once you have regained control over your mind you can return to the main object of the session.

A method recommended by Tibetan yogis is to imagine that the mind is enclosed within a tiny round seed whose upper hemisphere is white and lower red, situated in the central channel (see page 134) at the level of your navel. Concentrate on this until the mind has quietened down, then return to the object of meditation.

If you are familiar with the analytical meditations on death, impermanence or suffering (see Part Four), think briefly over the essential points of any one of these; this often helps to make your mind more calm and balanced. It might also help to recall your motivation – why you sat down to meditate in the first place – and thus strengthen your determination.

If mental excitement is a recurring problem, check your posture. The spine should be very straight and the head tilted slightly forward with the chin tucked slightly in – the mind tends to be restless when the head is raised too high. Reducing the amount of light in the room could also help, as bright light can stir up thoughts and feelings.

Patience is essential in dealing with a busy mind. Don't be upset with yourself if you can't keep your attention on the object of meditation. It takes time and persistent practice to learn to slow down and gain some control over the mind, so be easy on yourself.

Sleepiness

The very opposite of excitement is sleepiness. This can vary from a dull, listless state of mind to near-unconsciousness. It is related to another of our habits: usually, when we close our eyes and relax our mind and body, it's time to go to sleep!

First, make sure that your back is straight and your head is not bent forward too far. Open your eyes half-way and meditate with your gaze directed at the floor in front of you. Increasing the amount of light in the room should also help you to stay alert.

Another solution is to visualize your mind enclosed within a tiny seed in the central channel at the level of your naval, as before. This time, imagine that the seed shoots up the central channel and out through the crown of your head. The seed opens and your mind merges with vast, empty space. Concentrate on this experience for a while, then return to the meditation.

It is possible that sleepiness during meditation is symptomatic of underlying depression, in which case experimenting with some of the antidotes to depression on page 106 might help.

If your mind is still dull and sleepy after having tried these remedies, it would be best to either take a break or stop the meditation altogether.

Physical discomfort

Your meditations will flow smoothly if your body is relaxed and comfortable, but often it is difficult to get it into that state. Much of our physical tension is mind-related, arising from unresolved problems, fears, worries or anger. The most effective solution is to recognize these problems and settle them in meditation. A short-term method for easing physical tension – to be used either at the beginning of a meditation session or during it – is to sweep the body with your attention. Start at the top of the head and travel downwards through the body. Concentrate briefly on each part and consciously let it relax. Imagine that the tension simply dissolves.

Another method is to breathe deeply and slowly, and with much concentration imagine that the tension or pain leaves your body with each exhalation.

If neither of these methods works, you could try a more elaborate one: visualizing your body as hollow. Starting at the centre of your chest, imagine that all the internal, solid parts of your body dissolve into light, and then into empty space. Everything within your chest, head, arms and legs gradually dissolves and becomes empty. Your skin transforms into a very thin membrane of light to enclose this empty space. Concentrate for a while on this experience of your body being hollow, like a balloon.

If sitting causes discomfort or pain – in the knees or back, for example – it is all right to change to a more comfortable position. As meditation is an activity of the mind, not the body, it is more important to keep the mind clear and comfortable. However, at times it is useful just to *observe* the pain, which is a conscious experience, a mental perception, and try to overcome the usual fearful reaction to it. Instead of giving it the label "pain," see it as just a sensation, another type of energy. Doing such analysis should give you more insight into the workings of your mind and help you develop more control over your physical reactions.

An extension of this method of dealing with physical pain is mentally to increase it as much as possible. Imagine it getting worse and worse. After a while, return to the original pain – which now appears much less painful than before!

Another method is to visualize the suffering of all the beings of the universe and then, with great compassion, bring it mentally into the pain you are experiencing now. Meditate that you have taken on the pain of all beings, who are thus freed of all their suffering. Hold this thought and rejoice in it for as long as you can.

It is good to experiment with these methods for dealing with pain – but be careful not to overdo them and cause yourself an injury!

Strange images and sensations

Meditators sometimes experience unusual images appearing in the mind, or sensations such as the body expanding or shrinking, or the mind floating outside the body. These are normal reactions of the mind adjusting itself to a new activity and nothing to worry about.

On the other hand, do not be attached to such experiences or try to repeat them – this will only distract you from the real purpose of meditation. Simply observe whatever images or feelings arise without clinging to or rejecting them and let them disappear of their own accord.

However, if any disturbing experience occurs frequently

and you are unable to free yourself from it, you should consult a meditation teacher or a more experienced practitioner. It might be best to discontinue your practice until you receive their advice.

Discouragement

We often hear people complain, "I can't meditate; I've tried but it doesn't work," or "I've been meditating for so many months but nothing is happening." However, the problem is usually that they are expecting too much too quickly.

We need to be realistic. Most of us have never in our lives tried to understand our mind or control our thoughts and feelings. Old habits are not easy to break. Even if the results of daily meditation don't appear for two or three years – although this is highly unlikely – it should not be a cause for worry or despair.

Positive changes do not appear suddenly out of the blue, but develop slowly, gradually, little by little each day, so be patient with yourself. Remember, just making an effort to understand and control the mind *is* meditation. Trying to do what is best for yourself and others, you can feel confident that your meditation is worthwhile.

Often, new meditators think that their negative minds are getting worse, not better! And they feel that it is meditation that has caused it. Consider, however, what happens when you wash clothes. When you first put them into water, a certain amount of dirt comes out. As you continue to scrub them the water gets dirtier and dirtier. You might even be surprised by the amount of dirt that they contained. It would be foolish to blame the soap, water and scrubbing for the dirt – the process of washing merely reveals what is there already and is the right method for completely removing the dirt.

Similarly, meditation is the way to purify the mind of what is already there: at first we discover the gross negativities, then the more subtle.

So, be patient and don't worry!

Part Three
Meditations
on the Mind

1 *Breathing Meditations*

The principal mental activity used in breathing meditations is mindfulness, the ability of the mind to keep attention focused on whatever it is doing without forgetting it or wandering to other objects. Here, the object of concentration is one's own breath. In its most effective form mindfulness is accompanied by discriminating alertness, another function of the mind, which, like a sentry, watches out for distractions and disturbing thoughts.

Mindfulness is essential for successful meditation; and in our day-to-day lives it keeps us centred, alert and conscientious, helping us to know what is happening in our mind *as it happens* and thus to deal skilfully with problems as they arise.

There are various methods for cultivating mindfulness taught in different traditions; two variations are explained here. Choose the one you feel comfortable with and practise it consistently – it is best not to switch from one to the other.

You can use a breathing – or mindfulness – meditation either for your main practice or as a preliminary to other meditations. It is an invaluable technique: regular practice helps you gradually gain control over your mind. You will feel more relaxed and more able to enjoy life, having greater sensitivity to yourself and the people and things around you.

And using your increased mindfulness in other meditations, you will be able to maintain your concentration for longer periods.

Mindfulness meditation is therefore important for both beginners and advanced meditators: for those who want a simple technique for relaxing and calming the mind and for serious meditators who devote their lives to spiritual development.

THE PRACTICE

Sit with a straight back and relax your body. Bring to mind your motivation, or purpose, for doing this meditation, and decide that for the duration of the session you will keep your attention on the object of concentration in order to fulfil this purpose.

Choose one of the following methods of practising mindfulness of the breath.

1. Focus on the sensation at the tip of the nostrils as the breath enters and leaves your body. Keep your attention on this subtle perception and observe the full duration of each inhalation and exhalation.

If you like, you can count in cycles of five or ten complete breaths, starting again at one whenever you lose count or your mind wanders.

2. Use the method just described, but focus instead on the rising and falling of the abdomen with each inhalation and exhalation.

Whichever method you choose, breath normally and gently. Inevitably, thoughts will appear, but maintain a neutral attitude towards them, being neither attracted nor repulsed. In other words, do not react with dislike, worry, excitement or clinging to any thought, image or feeling that arises. Merely notice its existence and return your attention to the object of the meditation. Even if you have to do this fifty times a minute, don't feel frustrated! Be patient and persistent; eventually your thoughts will subside.

Imagine that your mind is like a calm, clear lake or a vast, empty sky: ripples appear on the surface of the lake and clouds pass across the sky, but they soon disappear without altering the natural stillness. Thoughts come and go; they are transient, momentary. Notice them and let them go, returning your attention again and again to the breath.

Be content to stay in the present. Accept whatever frame of mind you are in and whatever arises in your mind. Be free of expectation, clinging and frustration. Have no wish to be somewhere else, to be doing something else or even to feel some other way. Be content, just as you are.

When your skill has developed and your ability to avoid distractions increased, take your alertness a step further. Make mental notes of the nature of the thoughts that arise, such as "thinking of my friend," "thinking about breakfast," "hearing a bird," "feeling angry," "feeling bored." Simpler still, you can note "fantasy," "attachment," "memory," "sound," "pain." As soon as you have noted the thought or feeling, let it go, recalling its impermanent nature.

Another technique is to use your distractions to help you gain insight into the nature of the mind. When a thought arises, instead of focusing on the thought itself, focus on the thinker. This means that one part of the mind, discriminating alertness, takes a look at another part, a distraction. The disturbing object will disappear, but hold your attention on the thinker for as long as you can. Again, when another thought comes, focus on the thinker and follow the same procedure. Return to watching the breath once the distractions have passed.

These methods for handling distractions can be applied to any meditation. It is no use ignoring or suppressing disturbing thoughts or negative energy, because they will recur persistently. (For other methods for dealing with negative energy, see page 97.)

At the conclusion of your session, dedicate the positive energy created by your meditation to the fulfilment of whatever aim you started with.

2 Meditation on the Clarity of the Mind

The reality of our existence is that we are a combination of body and mind. Each of these in turn is a combination of many parts, all constantly in a state of flux. Unfortunately, our ego is not satisfied with such a simple explanation. It complicates matters by fabricating a view of an I or self based on our conceptions, likes and dislikes. We think, "I'm attractive," "I'm ugly," "I'm a good dancer," "I won't succeed," "I have a bad temper." We believe these projections and assume they are permanent and unchanging.

We do the same with people and objects in the world around us. We *believe* "he is ugly," "she is good." We build up our own elaborate and very solid picture of reality and hold on to it unquestioningly.

Meditation on the clarity of the mind is an effective antidote to our concrete projections. We can gain a direct experience of the clear, non-material, transient nature of all thoughts, feelings and perceptions, thus weakening the tendency to identify with them. As the subject – the mind – softens, so too do its projected objects; they slowly lose their concreteness. The feeling of dislike towards the "bad person" may still arise through habit, but we have the space to recall, "This is a projection of my thought, which is clear and transitory. It rises like a wave in my mind and soon will pass. The object does not exist in the way I see it."

This meditation is especially effective for softening our view of our own self. Normally our self-esteem is low, based on past mistakes, personality faults, bad habits and the like. But anger, jealousy, selfishness, depression and the other problems that haunt us are *mental* experiences and therefore clear and transitory. These states of mind *depend* for their existence on our belief in them! By recognizing this in meditation on the mind's nature we learn to let go of and stop identifying with these experiences.

Our intrinsic nature is clear and pure and is with us twenty-four hours a day. The negativities that rise and fall like waves on the ocean of our consciousness are temporary and can be eliminated. Consistent practice of this meditation will eventually generate a certainty about this pure nature to the point where it becomes our reality, our actual experience. This is a natural step towards understanding the more subtle nature of self and all phenomena: their emptiness of inherent existence (see page 58).

THE PRACTICE

Begin by breathing in deeply through both nostrils, bringing the air down to the stomach, holding it for a moment and then exhaling slowly and gently through your pursed lips. Repeat this twice, then breath normally; observe your breathing without thinking, without conceptualizing. Once your awareness has become sharp, turn your attention to the clarity of your consciousness.

Your consciousness, or mind, is whatever you are experiencing at the moment: sensations in your body, thoughts, feelings, perceptions of sounds and so forth. The nature of each of these experiences is clarity, without form or colour, space-like, pure awareness. Focus your attention on this clear, pure nature of the mind.

Initially it might be difficult to find the actual object, that is, the clarity. If so, meditate on a mental image of clarity – one way to generate such an image is to visualize space. Imagine lying on a hilltop and staring up at a sky that is completely clear and free of clouds. Concentrate on this vast, unobstructed emptiness. Imagine that it flows down and embraces you and your surroundings; everything becomes empty like space. Hold this experience; feel that the nature of your mind is like this clear, empty space.

Thoughts and distractions will arise, but do not react to them; neither follow them nor reject them. Remember that they are clear by nature, without substance. Simply watch them come and go, then return to the awareness of the mind's clarity.

Do not think about anything during this meditation. There is no need to wonder what the mind is; simply *observe* it, its clear nature, which is like infinite, empty space. That is sufficient. Be natural. Meditation is simple and natural; it is nothing special.

Concentration means holding the mind on an object continuously, without forgetting it. The automatic result of concentration is awareness, which is free of concepts. A light does not need to think, "I am dispelling darkness" – it simply illuminates. Awareness is an inner light that enables us to see things more clearly. It dispels the heaviness of how things appear to us, thus weakening our clinging or aversion to them.

Meditate for short periods – ten to thirty minutes – until your concentration has improved. Then you can sit for an hour or more, or as long as you can maintain strong awareness. If the meditation is going well, you will feel light and relaxed.

Conclude the meditation session by dedicating the positive energy created during it to the happiness and welfare of everyone.

3   *Meditation on the Continuity of the Mind*

The mind has been compared to a vast ocean, and our perceptions, thoughts and emotions to waves rising and falling on its surface. This analogy helps us to understand the experiences that occur while we are meditating or going about our daily activities. But to get a feeling for where the mind comes from and where it goes to, it is useful to think of it as a river, flowing through time.

Each moment of mind leads uninterruptedly to the next. The mind flows along ceaselessly, day and night, a stream of countless momentary experiences, always changing. Thoughts and feelings arise and quickly disappear, but they leave imprints that are carried on the mind-stream.

Buddhism explains that the mind is without beginning or end, unlike the body, which is conceived, born, dies and disintegrates. Our personality and experiences of this life are shaped by the imprints carried on the mind from past lives. Likewise, whatever we do and think now determines our future experiences. It is up to us: we can be whatever we want as long as we channel our energies in that direction. To do this we need to understand the mind and learn how to use it skilfully.

Accepting the existence of other lives hinges on under-standing the mind in this way. If you have been able to recall experiences from past lives you will realize that just as this life is the future of those past, so too will it be a past life of those to come. When your mind has become sufficiently calm you will be able to see deeply into it, and only when you have experienced the reality of past lives for yourself will you be convinced of their existence.

However, for many people it is an alien idea. Here are several analytical approaches to considering the validity of mental continuity.

First, the mind is impermanent, transitory, changing from moment to moment. Thus it is an effect, a result – the product of a cause. As a series of ever-changing moments, each necessarily the result of a previous moment, how could it have a beginning in time?

Some people hold that the mind is the brain. But as defined here, the mind is the experiences themselves – and how can a very thought or feeling be something physical? The mind *depends* upon the brain, and the nervous system, but cannot itself *be* the brain.

Nor can one's mind be derived from the minds of others, such as one's parents. If everything we are now and experi-ence now is necessarily the result of our past actions of body, speech and mind, then the mind must exist as the continuity of the individual alone.

The meditation here is very helpful for experiencing our own mind as a continuously-flowing, ever-changing stream of events.

THE PRACTICE

Sit comfortably and relax. Contemplate a positive, beneficial motivation for doing the meditation. Spend some time con-centrating on your breath, until the mind is quiet and clear.

First, take a look at your present state of mind, at the thoughts and sensations flashing by. Just observe them in a detached way, without clinging to or rejecting any of them.

Now, start to travel backwards through time. Briefly skim over the conscious experiences you have had since waking up this morning…. Are these part of the same stream of consciousness as your present experiences?

Before waking up, you were probably dreaming. Try to recall last night's dreams…. Do they also belong to this same mind-stream?

Continue to trace your mental experiences to yesterday, two days ago, last week, last month, last year; two, five, ten years ago. Continue to check if these experiences are of the same stream of consciousness.

Avoid getting involved in any of your recollections. The purpose of the meditation is not to relive good times or sort out problems from the past, but to get a feeling for the mind's continuity. If you should find something in your memory that you would like to investigate further, put it aside until later.

Go back in your life as far as you can, bringing to mind experiences from your adolescence and childhood…. People are sometimes able to remember their infancy, or even the time of birth. Relax and open your mind to allow such memories to arise…. You might even be able to recall something from another life.

Having reached back into your memory as far as you can, now gently bring your awareness into the present and again observe the thoughts and feelings that arise. Simply experience your stream of consciousness as it continues to flow; feel its momentum: one thought or feeling leading to the next, which leads to the next, which leads to the next, on and on.

Finally, try to get some idea of where it goes from here. Contemplate your mind-stream flowing through the rest of the day, and then tomorrow, the coming days, weeks and years ... up until death. What happens then?

Consider the different possibilities: does the stream of consciousness suddenly cease to exist? Does it transform into something else? Does it continue on, encountering new experiences?

Consider these possibilities carefully, using the reasons given earlier. Although you might not come to any definite conclusion, the important thing is to look with a clear mind. Finally, dedicate any insight you have gained to your eventual understanding of your mind for the sake of all living beings.

Part Four
Analytical
Meditations

About Analytical Meditation

The meditations presented here are solutions to a wide variety of problems and will help you develop a more realistic view of your inner and outer worlds.

A meditation on emptiness is given first, as this is the most powerful remedy to any difficulty. However, it might take time to develop sufficient grasp of this method for it to prove effective in dealing with strong, prevalent delusions. But persevere: it is well worthwhile.

The other meditations get us to look at our assumptions about life, suffering, death and human relationships and to see that it is these assumptions and their attendant expectations that cause our unhappiness and frustrations.

The section on dealing with negative energy gives advice on how to handle problems as they occur in day-to-day life.

Begin the meditations with a few minutes – or as long as you like – of breathing meditation, slowing down the mind and observing its present state.

Then, start the analysis. Do not let your mind wander from the subject you are analyzing: the more concentrated you are, the better. Dissolve your mind in the subject, penetrating it with intellectual thought, questions, images and illustrations from your own experience. Your meditation might take the form of an internal lecture, as though you were explaining a point to yourself; a debate, with yourself taking both sides; or a freestyle thought-adventure.

Doubts will inevitably arise, but do not gloss over them. Doubts are questions and questions need answers, so be clear about what you think, and why. Either come to a conclusion about the point in question or leave it aside for the moment and tackle it again later.

If during the analysis you should develop an intuitive experience of the subject, stop analyzing and hold the feeling with single-pointed concentration for as long as possible. When the feeling fades, resume the investigation or conclude the session. This union of analytical and stabilizing meditations is essential if we are to achieve true mind-transformation. In analytical meditation we think about and understand intellectually a particular point, and through stabilization meditation we gradually make it a part of our very experience of life.

1 Meditation on Emptiness

All Buddhist teachings are for the purpose of leading one gradually to the realization of emptiness. Here, emptiness means the emptiness of inherent, concrete existence, and the total eradication from our mind of this false way of seeing things marks our achievement of enlightenment, buddhahood.

What *is* "emptiness of inherent existence"? In practical terms, what does it mean? So-called inherent existence – of which all things are said to be empty – is a quality that we instinctively project onto every person and everything we experience. We see things as fully, solidly existing in and of themselves, from their own side, having their own nature, quite independent of any other cause and condition or of our own mind experiencing them.

Take a table, for example. We see a solid, independent table standing there, so obviously a table that it seems ridiculous to even question it. But where is the table? Where is its tableness located? Is it one of its legs? Or its top? Is it one of its parts? Or even one of its atoms? When did it start to be a table? How many parts do you take away before it ceases to be a table?

If you investigate thoroughly, you will discover that you simply cannot *find* the table you think is there. There is, however, an interdependent, changing from moment to moment, non-inherent table but this is not what we see. This is the crux of the problem. We experience not the bare reality of each thing and each person but an exaggerated, filled-out image of it projected by our own mind. This mistake marks every one of our mental experiences, is quite instinctive and is the very root of all our problems.

This pervasive mental disorder starts with the misapprehension of our own self. We are a composite of body – a mass of flesh, bones and skin – and mind – a stream of thoughts, feelings and perceptions. The composite is conveniently known as "Mary," "Harold," "woman," "man." It is a temporary alliance that ends with the death of the body and the flowing on of the mind to other experiences.

These stark, unembellished facts can be rather disquieting. A part of us, the ego, craving security and immortality, invents an inherent, independent, permanent self. This is not a deliberate, conscious process but one that takes place deep in our sub-conscious mind.

This fantasized self appears especially strongly at times of stress, excitement or fear. For example, when we narrowly escape an accident there is a powerful sense of an I that nearly suffered death or pain and must be protected. *That* I does not exist; it is an hallucination.

Our adherence to this false I – known as self-grasping ignorance – taints all our dealings with the world. We are attracted to people, places and situations that gratify and uphold our self-image, and react with fear or animosity to whatever threatens it. We view all people and things as definitely this way or that. Thus this root, self-grasping, branches out into attachment, jealousy, anger, arrogance, depression and the myriad other turbulent and unhappy states of mind.

The final solution is to eliminate this root ignorance with the wisdom that realizes the emptiness, in everything we experience, of the false qualities we project onto them. This is the ultimate transformation of mind.

Emptiness sounds pretty abstract but in fact is very practical and relevant to our lives. The first step towards understanding it is to try and get an idea of what it is we *think* exists; to locate, for example, the I that we believe in so strongly and then, by using clear reasoning in analytical meditation, to see that it is a mere fabrication, that it is something that has never existed and could never exist in the first place.

But don't throw out too much! You definitely exist! There *is* a conventional, interdependent self that experiences happiness and suffering, that works, studies, eats, sleeps, meditates and becomes enlightened. The first, most difficult task is to distinguish between this valid I and the fabricated one; usually we cannot tell them apart. In the concentration of meditation it is possible to see the difference; to recognize the illusory I and eradicate our long-habituated belief in it. The meditation here is a practical first step in that direction.

THE PRACTICE

Begin with a breathing meditation to relax and calm your mind. Motivate strongly to do this meditation in order to finally become enlightened for the sake of all beings.

Now, with the alertness of a spy, slowly and carefully become aware of the I. Who or what is thinking, feeling and meditating? How does it seem to come into existence? How does it appear to you? Is your I a creation of your mind? Or is it something existing concretely and independently, in its own right?

If you think you can identify it, try to locate it. Where is this I? Is it in your head...in your eyes...in your heart...in your hands...in your stomach...in your feet? Carefully consider each part of your body, including the organs, blood vessels and nerves. Can you find your I? It might be very small and subtle, so consider the cells, the atoms, the parts of the atoms.

After considering the entire body, again ask yourself how your I manifests its apparent existence. Does it still appear to be vivid and concrete? Is your body the I or not?

Perhaps you think your mind is the I. The mind is a constantly changing stream of thoughts, feelings and other experiences, coming and going in rapid alternation. Which of these is the I? Is it a loving thought...an angry thought...a happy feeling...a depressed feeling? Is your I the meditating mind... the dreaming mind? Can you find the I in your mind?

Is there any other place to look for your I? Could it exist somewhere else or in some other way? Examine every possibility you can think of.

Again, look at the way your I actually appears, feels to you. After this search for the I, do you notice any change? Do you still believe that it is as solid and real as you felt before? Does it still appear to exist independently, in and of itself?

Next, mentally disintegrate your body. Imagine all the atoms separating and floating apart. Billions and billions of minute particles scatter throughout space. Imagine that you can actually see this.

Now, disintegrate your mind. Let every thought, feeling, sensation and perception float away.

Stay in this experience of space without being distracted by thoughts. When the feeling of an independent, inherent I recurs, analyze it again. Does it exist in the body? In the mind? How does it exist?

Do not make the mistake of thinking, "My body is not the I and my mind is not the I, therefore I don't exist." You *do* exist, but not in the way you instinctively feel, that is as independent and inherent. Conventionally, your self exists *in dependence upon* mind and body, and this combination is the basis to which conceptual thinking ascribes a name: "I" or "self" or "Mary" or "Harold." This is the you that is sitting and meditating and wondering, "Maybe I don't exist"!

Whatever exists is necessarily dependent upon causes and conditions, or parts and names, for its existence. This is how things exist conventionally, and understanding interdependence is the principal cause for understanding a thing's ultimate nature, its emptiness. The conventional nature of something is its dependence upon causes and conditions and its ultimate nature is its emptiness of inherent, independent existence.

Think now about how your body exists conventionally: *in dependence upon* skin, blood, bones, legs, arms, organs and so forth. In turn, each of these exists *in dependence upon* their own parts: cells, atoms, and sub-atomic particles.

Think about your mind, how it exists *in dependence upon* thoughts, feelings, perceptions, sensations. And how, in turn, each of these exists *in dependence upon* the previous conscious experiences that gave rise to them.

Now, go back to your feeling of self or I. Think about how *you* exist conventionally, *in dependence upon* mind and body and name – the self's parts.

When the body feels hungry or cold, for example, you think "I am hungry," "I am cold." When the mind has an idea about something, you say "I think." When you feel love for someone you say "I love you." When introducing yourself to someone you say "I am so-and-so."

Apart from this sense of I that depends upon the ever-flowing, ever-changing streams of body and mind, is there an I that is solid, unchanging and independent?

The mere absence of such an inherently-existing I is the emptiness of the self.

Finish the session with a conclusion as to how you, your *self*, exists. Conclude by dedicating sincerely any positive energy and insight you have gained to the enlightenment of all beings. Think that this meditation is just one step along the path to finally achieving direct insight into emptiness and thus cutting the root of suffering and dissatisfaction.

2   *Appreciating our Human Life*

The function of analytical meditation is to help us recognize and cut through the mistaken attitudes and ideas that cause unhappiness and dissatisfaction. Our experiences in life depend upon how we think and feel about things, and because most of the time we do not perceive things the way they really are, we encounter one frustrating situation after another.

As long as we blame our parents, society or other external factors, we will never find any satisfying solutions to our problems. Their main cause lies within our own mind, so we need to take responsibility for changing our way of thinking where it is mistaken, that is, where it brings unhappiness to ourselves and others.

This can be done through meditation, by gradually becoming aware of how we think and feel, distinguishing correct from incorrect attitudes, and finally counteracting harmful attitudes by the appropriate means.

The starting-point for many problems is the way we feel about ourselves and our life. Human existence is very precious, but normally we fail to appreciate it. We have so much potential, so much latent wisdom and loving kindness, so much to offer the world, but we ignore this and let ourselves become clouded with depression. Focusing on shortcomings in our character and failings in our dealings with people and work, for example, we develop an unfair, low opinion of ourselves. This self-image becomes more and more concrete with time. We identify ourselves as incapable and inadequate, and consequently turn to other people in an attempt to find happiness and fulfilment. However, as our friends are likely to feel the same way about themselves, such relationships often bring only more frustration.

We can unlock the potential for happiness and satisfaction that lies within each of us by becoming aware of our mental processes, and then applying discriminating wisdom to all our actions of body, speech and mind. But to hope to be able to achieve this and, through it, fulfilment without first completing the necessary groundwork is to invite frustration. We must start by building a firm foundation, based on a realistic view of ourselves. We have to accept our positive as well as our negative traits, and determine to nourish the good and transform or eliminate the bad aspects of our character. Eventually we will recognize how fortunate we are to have been born human. Once we understand this, we can begin to train our minds to achieve enlightenment.

When we look at ourselves deeply, carefully, we find that most of our day-to-day problems are quite trivial. It is only our projections and conceptions that complicate them and allow them to grow out of all proportion. As we self-indulgently become caught up in our problems, they appear to grow larger and larger, and we disappear into deep states of depression and hopelessness. Wallowing in self-pity, we are unable to see that, in fact, we have created our problems and, therefore, our depressive state.

This meditation is an antidote to negative states of being such as depression and hopelessness. It helps us to recognize and rejoice in our good fortune, in our extraordinary and unique potential to achieve true happiness and satisfaction. An understanding of this potential naturally fills us with joy and enthusiasm for life – who wouldn't feel elated at the realization that they hold the key to their own fulfilment? At the same time, recognizing our good fortune helps us to see clearly that there are many who are infinitely less fortunate than we are. We feel true compassion for them and take an active concern in their plight.

THE PRACTICE

Start with mindfulness meditation on the breath in order to bring your mind to a clear, calm state. Feel free to spend as much time as you like doing this.

Then begin the analytical meditation by checking up on how you feel about yourself: your life, personality, accomplishments, abilities, and so forth. Are you satisfied or do you find many faults, much to be desired? Can you detect feelings of inadequacy, discouragement or hopelessness? Even if your present state of mind is positive and things are going well for you, recall past times of depression and discouragement. Determine to get rid of this dark sense of hopelessness.

To help you develop a better perspective on your own life, first compare it with the lives of others worse off than you. Try to imagine what it would be like as an animal, for example: deeply ignorant, with no potential for mental and spiritual development; controlled by others; experiencing the perpetual round of hunger, thirst, heat and cold, and living always in fear of death.

Imagine being a beggar on the streets of Calcutta or living in the deserts of Africa, constantly in need of food and water with no time to think of anything else; human, but with little more opportunity for development than an animal.

Imagine having severe mental or physical handicaps, and

the lack of freedom this would mean. Or imagine living in a country where there is political and social oppression, allowing you little freedom to pursue your interests.

It is easy enough to read and repeat these words, but to really put yourself in one of these situations is another matter. Visualizing and thinking deeply about the plight of the beggar, the fear and paranoia of an animal, the hopelessness of the person in the desert, can be very frightening and painful. But by understanding the agony of each of these situations we learn to appreciate how miniscule our present problems are. Compare your problems to what others undergo; be thankful for what you have and feel compassion for others' hardships.

Now bring to mind all the good qualities and advantages of your life. You are a human being with an intelligent mind, loving heart and healthy body. Your friends and family support you. You have the good fortune to live in a country comparatively free of social and political oppression. You have countless opportunities to pursue your creative, intellectual and social interests; opportunities to go anywhere and do anything. You enjoy a good standard of living. And most of all you have the potential and opportunity – *because* of all the other benefits – to investigate, understand and transform your mind.

Think now how few people or creatures on earth share these freedoms and chances with you. When you have considered this deeply, you will realize how rare and precious a life like yours is. Really appreciate your good fortune.

Once you have seen the disadvantages your life is free of and the advantages you enjoy, you must decide how best to use your precious opportunities. Think of all the possibilities open to you – work, travel, enjoyment, study. And these are simply the mundane opportunities. The greatest benefit this life can bring is the chance for spiritual development, transformation of your mind.

Try to see the limitations of a lifestyle geared solely to materialistic gain. Think of the insignificance of fame, wealth, reputation, sensual indulgence when compared to the goal of enlightenment. Why aspire to only temporal achievements when we are capable of so much more?

Contemplate all these points slowly and carefully. Look at them from various angles. Your power to control your mind and, through it, to achieve enlightenment should become clear. How, with such power, can you possibly feel hopeless and depressed?

Dedicate the energy and inspiration you have gained from doing this meditation to the ultimate happiness of all beings.

3 Death Awareness Meditation

When first confronted with the idea of meditating on death we might react with shock. Perhaps we think that meditation should deal with good experiences, whereas death and things associated with it – tears of grief, black clothing, skeletons and cemeteries – evoke feelings of fear and panic. We see death as the contradiction of life, beauty and happiness; it belongs to the realm of the unmentionable, the unthinkable.

But why do we have such unrealistic attitudes? Why are we unable to accept death as calmly as we accept yesterday's fresh flowers wilting today? Change, disintegration and death are natural, inevitable aspects of existence.

Buddhism explains death as the separation of mind and body, after which the body disintegrates and the consciousness continues to another life. The conventional self, or I, that depends on the present mind-body combination ends at death, but a different self-image will arise with the new life. Death is therefore not a cessation but a transition, a transformation.

At the root of our uneasiness and denial is ignorance. We cling to our self-image as something permanent and unchanging, and want it to live forever. This wish may not be conscious, expressible in thoughts or words, but it is definitely there; it accounts for why we instinctively flee, struggle or shield ourselves when our life is threatened.

This is not to imply that there is something wrong with trying to stay alive – life is indeed very precious. But it would be useful to examine the nature of the I that does not want to die. The fault is not in the wish to prolong life but in the fundamental idea of who or what we really are. "Am I the body, or any part of this collection of bones, blood and flesh?" "Am I my consciousness?" "Am I something other than my body and my mind?"

The understanding of emptiness, or the non-existence of an inherent, permanent self, frees us from fear of death and from *all* fears and misconceptions. Until that point is reached, however, it is important to maintain awareness of impermanence and death.

The principal benefit of practising this meditation is that it forces us to decide what attitudes and activities are truly worthwhile. Human life is highly significant because of the opportunities it provides for our spiritual growth: developing love and compassion, clarity and wisdom, and finally achieving enlightenment. Each of us has this potential.

But life is short. Death can happen at any time, and to die without having undertaken the only work that has any lasting benefit, either to ourselves or to others, would be highly regrettable. The present life and all its experiences are fleeting; clinging to anything in this world is like chasing a rainbow. If we keep this in mind constantly we will not waste time on mundane pursuits but spend it wisely, avoiding what is negative and thus the cause of unhappiness, and cultivating what is positive and thus the cause of happiness.

How we live our life inevitably affects how we die. If we live peacefully, we will die with peace, but if we fail to take death into consideration and thus fail to prepare for it, we are likely to die with fear and regret – states of mind that will only compound our suffering.

There is no need whatsoever to regard death with fear or sorrow. It can in fact be an enlightening experience, but whether or not it will be depends on how we live each day, each moment of our life. Awareness of death during life helps us to stay in the present, to see the past as dream-like and hopes for the future as fantasies. We will be more stable and content and will enthusiatically make the most of our life.

There are various ways of meditating on death; the one explained here involves contemplating nine points. For the main body of the meditation, contemplate in depth one of these, then briefly scan the others. If you do one session each day, after nine days you will have dealt with each topic at length and can begin again with the first.

The nine points are divided into three sections.

The inevitability of death

The uncertainty of the time of death

The fact that only your spiritual insight can help at the time of death

THE PRACTICE

As preparation, bring your mind to a calm, alert state and think clearly about your motivation for doing the meditation. You might like to recite some of the prayers on page 139.

Then, with your mind relaxed but fully concentrated, contemplate the subject, using analytical thought enriched with your own experiences and insights, in an effort to feel it deeply. Remember, if at any time during the session you reach a strong, intuitive experience of the point you are examining, hold the feeling with your attention as long as possible.

THE INEVITABILITY OF DEATH
1   *Everyone has to die*

We plan many projects and activities for the coming days, months and years. Although death is the only event that is certain to occur, we don't count it among our plans.

To generate an experience of death's inevitability, first bring to mind people from the past: famous rulers and writers, musicians, philosophers, saints, criminals, and ord-inary people. These people were once alive – they worked, thought and wrote; they loved and fought, enjoyed life and suffered. And finally they died.

Is there anyone who ever lived who did not have to die? No matter how wise, wealthy, powerful or popular a person may be, his or her life must come to an end. The same is true for all other living creatures. For all the advances in science and medicine, there is still no cure for death and no one expects to be able to eradicate it.

Now bring to mind all the people you know. Go through them one by one, reflecting that each of them will one day die.

Think of all the human beings on earth at the moment: one hundred years from now only a handful of these billions of people will still be alive. You yourself will be dead. Experi-ence this fact with your entire being.

2   *Your lifespan is decreasing continuously*

Even as you sit, time is passing. Seconds become minutes, minutes become hours, hours become days, days become years, and you travel closer and closer towards death. Hold your awareness for a while on the experience of this uninter-rupted flow of time carrying you to the end of your life.

If you were to fall from an aeroplane without a parachute you would be fully aware of death's approach. Imagine this is actually happening to you, and check what thoughts and feelings pass through your mind.

The reality of your situation in life in not so different: you are constantly moving towards death and can do nothing to avoid or postpone it.

3   *The amount of time spent during your life to develop your mind is very small*

Given that the mind alone continues after death, the only thing that will be of any value when you die is the positive and constructive energy you have created during your life. But how much time do you actually devote to understanding your mind, being kind to others, developing wisdom and compassion?

In an average day, how many hours do you sleep? How many hours do you work? How many hours do you spend eating, socializing? How much time do you spend feeling depressed, frustrated, bored, angry, resentful, jealous, lazy or critical? And finally, how much time do you spend consciously trying to improve your state of mind?

Do these calculations honestly. Assess your life in this practical way to see clearly just how much of your time is spent doing things that will bring positive results, that is, happiness for yourself and others.

By meditating on these first three points we will develop the determination to use our life wisely and mindfully.

THE UNCERTAINTY OF THE TIME OF DEATH
4   *Human life-expectancy is uncertain*

If human beings died at a specific age, say eighty-eight, we would have plenty of time and space to prepare for death. But there is no such certainty, and death catches most of us by surprise.

Life can end at any point: at birth, in childhood, in adolescence, at the age of twenty-two or thirty-five or fifty or ninety-four. Even if we are now young and healthy, there is no guarantee that we will live much longer. We can *hope* to live until we are seventy or eighty, but we cannot be certain of doing so. We cannot be certain that we will not die later today.

It is very difficult to feel convinced that death could happen at any moment. We tend to feel that since we've survived so far, our continuation is secure. But thousands of people die every day and few of them expected to.

Generate a strong feeling of the complete uncertainty of

your own time of death; how there simply is no guarantee that you have long to live.

5 *There are many causes of death*

Daily, we hear of some disaster or other – volcanic eruptions and earthquakes, forest fires, storms and floods; war, famine and terrorism – bringing about the death of thousands of human beings.

For those of us who feel remote and safe from these kinds of violent death, there are the more day-to-day causes such as heart attacks, cancer and other fatal diseases; plane and car crashes; fires, drowning and murder. Even things that are meant to support and protect life can cause death: houses and hotels collapse or burn; food and medicine, if improperly taken, can lead to death. And then there is old age; no one is safe from that.

People die in their sleep, in the womb, coming home from work, going to school, on the playing field, cooking dinner. Death can occur at any time, in any situation. Contemplate this; see clearly that it is the nature of life on this planet, and that any one of the catalogue of causes can bring about your own death.

6 *The human body is so fragile*

The body is extremely vulnerable; it can wound and break so easily. Within minutes, it can change from being strong and active to being helplessly weak and full of pain.

Right now you might feel healthy, energetic and secure, but something as small as a virus or as insignificant as a thorn could drain your strength and lead to your death.

Think about this. Recall the times you have hurt or injured your body, and how easily it could happen again and even cause your death.

Your body won't last forever. In the course of your life you might manage to avoid illness and accidents, but the years will eventually overtake you – your body will degenerate, lose its beauty and vitality and finally die.

By meditating on these second three points we will develop the determination to begin our work of mind-transformation right now, as the future is so uncertain.

THE FACT THAT ONLY SPIRITUAL INSIGHT CAN HELP YOU AT THE TIME OF DEATH

No matter how much we have acquired or developed throughout our life – in terms of family and friends, wealth, power, travel experiences and so on – none of it goes with us at death. Only our stream of consciousness continues, carrying imprints of all that we have thought, felt, said and done. We should aim to die at peace with ourselves, feeling good about how we lived our life and not leaving behind any unresolved conflicts with people.

The only things that will truly benefit us at the time of death are the imprints left by our development of love, wisdom, patience, compassion and other positive attitudes. If we can realize this now, we will have the energy and determination to live a meaningful life.

You can experience a strong feeling of this reality by contemplating the following three points while visualizing yourself actually dying.

7   *Your possessions and enjoyments cannot help*

As you lie on your death-bed, your body growing weaker by the minute, where do your thoughts turn? When you are unhappy or ill you usually take refuge in material comforts, but can food, medicine, sleep, music, drugs or alcohol help you now?

Think of your possessions, all those things you have made such an effort to acquire in order to fulfil your needs and desires: what can they do for you now?

Try to recognize your dependence upon these things and recall that you cannot take any of them with you. Not only are they unable to help you at death, your attachment to them will only be a hindrance to dying peacefully.

8 *Your loved ones cannot help*

You will turn for help especially to your loved ones, who have much concern and affection for you and have given you so much comfort and security. But now, as your consciousness is slipping away, there is little they can do for you. You are totally alone in your experience of death.

Clinging to loved ones and feeling grief at the thought of separating from them will create only turmoil in your mind and make a peaceful death impossible.

Recognize the attachment you have to your family and friends. Realize that it is utterly inappropriate to feel so strongly attached, both in life and at death.

9 *Your own body cannot help*

Your body has been your constant companion since birth. You know it more intimately than anything or anyone else. You have cared for it and protected it, worried about it, kept it comfortable and healthy, fed it and cleaned it, experienced all kinds of pleasure and pain with it. It has been your most treasured possession.

But now you are dying and that means you will be separated from it. It will become weak and eventually quite useless: you will leave it and it is destined for the cemetery. What good can it possibly do you now?

Contemplate the strong sense of dependence and attachment you have to your body and how it cannot benefit you in any way at death. Fear of pain and regret about leaving it will only compound your suffering.

By meditating on the final three points we will develop the determination to keep our life and practice of mind-transformation free from attachment to people and possessions.

It is possible you will feel depressed or worried after doing this meditation. In one sense this shows you have taken the ideas seriously and contemplated them well, but it also shows you have made a wrong conclusion, and it would not be wise to end your session in such a state of mind. Remember that death is just a natural and inevitable aspect of life, and it is your inability to accept it as such that makes you upset.

Fear and regret arise because of unrealistic clinging to a permanent self. If we keep death in mind in an easy, open way this clinging will loosen, allowing us to be mindful and make every action positive and beneficial, for ourselves and others. And an awareness of death gives us enormous energy to not waste our life but to live it as effectively as possible.

Conclude the meditation with the optimistic thought that you have every possibility to make your life meaningful and positive and thus will be able to die with peace of mind.

4   *Meditation on Impermanence*

Everything in the physical world is impermanent, changing all the time. Some changes are obvious: people grow up, get old and die; buildings and bridges wear out and fall apart. The environment goes through a complete transformation from one season to the next; flowers wilt, paint cracks and peels, cars break down.

The source of this external transformation can be traced to the cellular and molecular composition of matter, where change is not so obvious. At this invisible level, minute particles are constantly coming into or going out of existence, gathering and dispersing, expanding and contracting – always in motion, always fluctuating.

Our conscious world is also changing constantly. Sometimes we are happy, sometimes depressed; sometimes we feel full of love, other times full of anger. Memories of conversations and events, thoughts of the future, ideas about this and that fill our minds one after the other. A few moments of looking inward will show us how quickly the mind is changing: it's like a railway station at rush hour! Streams of thoughts, feelings and perceptions flash by, in every direction, without ceasing.

This constant change is the reality of things, but we find it very difficult to accept. Intellectually, it is not a problem; but real acceptance of impermanence rarely, if ever, enters our everyday behaviour and experience. Instinctively, we cling to people and things as if they were permanent and un-changing. We don't want the nice person or the beautiful object to change and firmly believe that the irritating person will never be different.

We cling especially stongly to our view of our own per-sonality: "I am a depressed person," "I am an angry person," "I am not very intelligent." We might indeed be this or that, but it is not the whole picture and nor will it always be like that; it will change.

By not recognizing impermanence we meet with frustra-tion, irritation, grief, loneliness and countless other problems. We can avoid experiencing them by becoming familiar with the transitory nature of things, recognizing that they are in a constant state of flux. Gradually we will learn to expect, and accept, change as the nature of life.

We will understand not only that change simply happens but also that we can bring about change. We have the power to change what we are, to develop and transform our minds and lives.

THE PRACTICE

Sit comfortably and relax completely. Take time to calm and concentrate your thoughts by mindfully observing the breath.

Become aware of your body. Think of its many different parts – arms, legs, head, skin, blood, bones, nerves and muscles. Examine them, one by one; *probe* them with your feelings. Contemplate the nature of these things: their sub-stance, their texture, their shape and size. Be sensitive to the body at work, the movement that is going on each moment: the ebb and flow of your breath, the beating of your heart, the flow of your blood and the energy of your nerve-impulses.

Be aware of your body at the even more subtle level of its

cellular structure, that it is entirely composed of living cells moving about, reproducing, dying and disintegrating.

Now, turn your attention to your mind. It, too, is composed of countless parts: thoughts, perceptions, feelings following one after the other, ceaselessly. Simply watch this ever-changing flow of mental experiences.

After contemplating your inner physical world in this way, now turn to the outer world. Slowly increase your awareness to include your immediate surroundings: picture in your mind the seat you are on, the walls and ceilings of your room, the space around you and the objects filling it. Consider that each of these, although appearing solid and static, is actually a mass of tiny particles whizzing around. Stay with that experience for a while.

Then continue to expand your awareness of subtle impermanence to take in the house or building you are in, trees, streets, people and animals, cars, cities and mountains – go as far as you like. Recall that each being or object you touch with your thoughts is, at a very subtle level, changing right now. Nothing remains the same from one moment to the next. Concentrate on this experience.

During the meditation, any time that you have a clear, strong feeling of the ever-changing nature of things, hold your attention firmly on it for as long as possible (in other words, do stabilizing meditation). Soak your mind in the experience. When the feeling fades or your attention starts to wander, again analyze the impermanence of either your body or mind or another object.

Conclude the meditation with the thought that it is unrealistic and self-defeating to cling to things as though they were permanent. Whatever is beautiful and pleasing will change and eventually disappear, so we can't expect it to give us lasting happiness. Also, whatever is unpleasant or disturbing won't last forever– it might even change for the better! – so there's no need to be upset, or to reject it.

Dedicate your positive energy and insight to the happiness of all living beings.

5   *Meditation on Suffering*

The question of suffering has always perplexed philosophers and theologians – not to mention ordinary suffering human beings like us! Why is there so much fighting in the world? Why so much starvation, sickness, inequality and injustice? What are the causes of suffering? The Buddhist view can be summarized as what are known as the four noble truths.

First, *suffering exists*. Every being in existence suffers to some degree or other.

Second, *suffering always has a cause*. The principal causes of suffering – of everything that we experience – are necessarily previous actions of our body, speech or mind.

Third, *there is an end to suffering*. We all have the potential to reach a state of perfect clarity and compassion, in which we no longer experience the results of past suffering or create the causes for future suffering.

Fourth, *there is a means to end suffering*. The way to end suffering is gradually to abandon its causes – anger, selfishness, attachment and other negative states of mind – and cultivate the causes of happiness – patience, love, non-attachment, generosity and the other positive states of mind. And finally, by developing insight into the true nature of all things, we can cut the very root of suffering altogether.

"Suffering" refers to all levels of physical and psychological experiences. There are many ways to meditate on suffering and all are for the purpose of generating a deep sense of its extensiveness; how, in varying degrees, it permeates our own lives and the lives of all others.

The purpose of developing this awareness is not to increase our misery. On the contrary, successful meditation on suffering brings us to a more realistic view of life. Gradually we will see that unravelling the complexities of our mind and developing control over our thoughts and actions is both desirable and possible.

Our usual view of life is unrealistic. Most of our pleasant experiences depend on external objects and situations, whose very nature is ephemeral. When these things do change or disappear we cling on, unwilling to accept the reality of the situation. We *want* pleasure to last and are disappointed when it doesn't. And so we go, up and down, from pleasure to pain and happiness to unhappiness, all our lives.

Awareness of this reality is a step towards eliminating suffering. We will stop expecting people and things to make us happy and instead see that it is our attitude towards them that determines happiness and satisfaction. Ironically, when we stop clinging unrealistically to things, we enjoy them all the more!

Another major benefit of this meditation is that we can see that others suffer in the same way, and as a result we inevitably develop more kindness and compassion towards them.

But the main purpose of recognizing the suffering of our lives is to develop the strong intention to do what is necessary to be finally free of it. All unhappy, painful experiences are rooted in the ignorance that believes everything exists inherently, in and of itself. Seeing the emptiness, the lack, of this way of existing cuts through all confusion and problems.

Gaining this understanding, however, is no simple matter. It requires tremendous energy to concentrate the mind on the nature of things, to cut through our habitual perception of them to reach their ultimate, pure reality. The fuel that drives us in this task is the desire to free ourselves, and others, from all suffering.

THE PRACTICE

Sit comfortably and relax. Check your motivation for doing the meditation.

There are three aspects of suffering to contemplate. Go through each as slowly as you like. Don't just make a mental checklist of the points but bring your emotions and intuition into the meditation; really *feel* each example of suffering as if you were experiencing it right now.

1   *The suffering of suffering*

This includes all obvious forms of suffering, physical and mental.

First, think of all the normal, everyday problems your body experiences: aches and pains, heat and cold, hunger and thirst, bad eyesight, earaches, cuts and burns, overweight, muscle tension, fatigue – the list is endless. Recall these experiences and how we are rarely without one or more of them.

Now think of the more extreme physical suffering you have experienced in the past and see the possibility of it happening again; there is no guarantee it will not.

Think of the physical suffering you will experience when you are old. Picture yourself at the age of eighty or ninety, your body degenerated and wrinkled and not functioning properly. Finally, there is death. Think of the different ways you could die and the suffering of the body then.

Contemplate the fact that, like every other material thing, it is the nature of the body to change, meet with pain, degenerate and eventually die. Therefore it is unrealistic and unwise to be attached to it.

Now bring your mind to mental and emotional suffering.

Recall past experiences of loneliness, depression, grief, frustration, jealousy, anger, fear, confusion, anxiety. Go back over your life and see that rarely was there a time when you were not experiencing at least some of these emotions. Relive them.

Now look at your present state of mind. Are you anxious? Depressed? Angry? Confused? Agitated? Think of the mental suffering that is likely to come in the future when people close to you die or leave you, and when you yourself die or when the myriad other things occur in our lives that are likely to cause unhappiness to one degree or another.

Expand your thoughts to include the experiences of others. At this very moment all beings in existence, simply because they have a confused mind and a perishable body, are going through some form of mental or physical pain – from the slightest discomfort to the grossest suffering.

Start with the people you know – your friends, relatives and neighbours. Some are sick, some old; others are depressed, anxious, dissatisfied, lonely. Then think about the people you don't know, whose lives are plagued by war, poverty, unemployment, racism, disease, political oppression.

We also share this world with animals and other creatures. Contemplate their day-to-day suffering: hunger, pain, cold, lack of freedom, fear of being killed.

Become aware that all of these countless living beings have a stream of consciousness not so different from your own: we all react with joy to kindness and beauty, with fear to pain and harm, and with anger to whatever threatens the peace of ourselves and our loved ones. We all try to be happy and to avoid problems, but as long as we are unenlightened we meet with one suffering situation after another.

2   *The suffering of change*

This more subtle level of suffering refers to the experiences that normally we think of as pleasure. They are called "suffering" because they do not last. Every nice experience come to an end without fully satisfying us and thus leads, instead, to the desire to repeat it, in the hope that we will find the satisfaction we think it should give us.

Think of any pleasurable experience; it is true for each. A nice meal, sex, a day at the beach, skiing, music, a movie, a cigarette, a beautiful sunset. Even sitting comfortably in a chair: eventually you need to change position because the comfort soon turns to discomfort. Or sitting by a fire on a chilly day: at first it is such a pleasure, but soon you must move away because it becomes too hot.

Look carefully at your life and see whether or not this is true. Recall some good experiences: did they last? Did they truly satisfy you? If the pleasure is true pleasure, why doesn't it stay with you indefinitely? Can you think of any example of unchangeable, lasting happiness in your life or in anyone else's?

Contemplate how everything changes; how experiences, no matter how pleasurable, do not last but lead inevitably to dissatisfaction, irritation, boredom or loneliness.

It is the very nature of all things that they change and eventually come to an end. Even a blissful relationship has its ups and downs and will finally end with death. Beautiful people grow old and grey and eventually die. Power does not last and wealth runs out. Flowers wither, sunsets fade, parties end.

Conclude this part of the meditation by firmly deciding that it is not reasonable to cling to any person or object as a means of finding lasting satisfaction; that, in fact, it brings the very opposite result.

3   *All-pervading suffering*

This is even more subtle than the suffering of change. It refers to our very existence as ordinary, unenlightened beings. Lacking the direct, intuitive insight into the true nature of things, we are caught in a bind: on the one hand, we experience in each moment the effects of previous causes and, on the other, we create each moment the causes for future effects. This very moment of existence is both the effect of past suffering and the cause of suffering in the future.

The fact of being stuck in this cycle, this complex web of problems, is itself all-pervading suffering. Let your mind absorb this idea. Generate a strong feeling for the self-perpetuating dilemma that is your existence.

Then contemplate how there are countless living beings caught up in this seemingly endless cycle, just as you are.

But don't panic. The situation is not hopeless! There is a way out of this cycle. As there is a cause – our false view of the way things exist – there is necessarily a cause of the end of this suffering, an antidote. The final antidote is to develop the right understanding of the nature of reality and thus cut through our confusion and our habit of following ego's whims.

In the meantime, we can use our life and energy in positive ways like helping others with love and generosity and counteracting harmful attitudes in our mind as they arise. As our understanding of reality grows, so too does our detachment from ordinary, transient things, and our web of confusion gradually untangles. Finally, this understanding becomes a direct, intuitive perception of emptiness, which eliminates, once and for all, the very root of suffering.

Draw conclusions from any insights you may have had during this meditation. Acknowledging the painful, dissatisfactory nature of life is quite difficult, but it is the only way out. Until we stop running away from the reality of suffering and learn to deal honestly with the rough, unsubdued aspects of our mind, we will continue to circle in confusion. Awareness of suffering gives us the energy we need to penetrate the nature of reality.

Thus, conclude your session optimistically, with the determination to use your life skilfully and do what you can to overcome suffering.

Dedicate all your good intentions and energy to the growth of insight in yourself and all others.

PRACTICAL APPLICATION

We have plenty of opportunities in our day-to-day lives to familiarize ourselves with the ideas presented in this meditation. Each day we experience a multitude of troubles: hunger, tiredness, aches and pains, irritation, boredom, frustration. Our usual reaction is to get rid of or by-pass these problems as quickly as possible. But it is a good idea – before reaching for a painkiller, turning on the TV, checking what's in the fridge or seeking out a friend – to spend a few minutes just *experiencing* the pain: "So, *this* is suffering!"

Because we habitually avoid confronting and dealing with pain, it is difficult in meditation to take a good, honest look at the reality of suffering. Therefore, we should learn to use our actual experiences, as they occur, to deepen our understanding of the subject.

This does not mean that we should regard life as one big tragedy or go around always miserable and tense. We can be aware of suffering and still keep a sense of humour. Happiness and suffering are both impermanent, transitory experiences. We should not emphasize one over the other, but acknowledge the changeable nature of both.

So, when we find ourselves grasping unrealistically to a new person in our life, say, we should remind ourselves that the happiness we're experiencing is transitory and cannot eliminate all our problems, anyway. With this attitude, which is more realistic and less exaggerated, we will probably enjoy the experience all the more!

When there is a problem, physical or psychological, we should think, "It's transitory – at some point it will be gone. But problems and suffering will continue to happen to me until I work on my mind and eliminate all causes of suffering." By doing this, the problem can become a teaching.

When people around us are suffering, we should be sensitive and compassionate and help them to the best of our ability. But we should not get so involved that their problem becomes our problem and we grow tense and worried over it. We can avoid this by recalling that the cause, and the solution, of any problem lie in the mind of the person experiencing it. It's up to them to work their way out of it. As long as we are loving and kind and do whatever we can to ease their pain, we should not feel guilty or inadequate and think we must do more.

6   *Equilibrium Meditation*

The goal of Mahayana practice is to reach the state of perfect wholeness, enlightenment, in order to help others achieve it too. The aspiration to do this is known as "the mind of enlightenment" (Sanskrit: *bodhicitta*), and is the experience of opening our heart to all beings, allowing love and compassion to flow to everyone, without limitation. A person who possesses bodhicitta actually feels responsible to ease the suffering of all living beings and lead them to happiness.

We can start to cultivate the mind of enlightenment now, in our day-to-day lives, by being kind and open to the people we meet: being patient with them and aware of their needs. It is easy, however, to deceive ourselves, to play the role of a friendly open person while hiding our feelings of irritation and intolerance. So it is important to get in touch with our feelings while also making an effort to extend ourselves to others, and this is done most effectively in the concentration of meditation.

Normally, we discriminate: we either like, dislike or are indifferent to everyone we meet. These reactions are mostly self-centred, based on whether the person appears agreeable, disagreeable or uninteresting to *me*.

At the root of this discrimination is our instinctive misunderstanding of the way things exist, especially our own self. This problem has always been with us and we build on it elaborately throughout life, thinking, and believing, "I am this way and will always be; this is good for me and that brings me down."

Our belief in this I gives rise to the desire to protect and nourish it. Everything we do is for the sake of this self. It has needs that must be fulfilled; it must find happiness and avoid pain. The I likes this person because she makes it happy and dislikes that person because he causes it pain. Everything is seen from the perspective of this I's needs.

Our basic misapprehension of the I makes our perception faulty. If we analyze and search for the permanent, fixed self that seems to be there, we cannot find it; it is an illusion. There is only a fluctuating stream of mind and body travelling through life, experiencing joy, problems, love, frustration. We meet people, interact with them briefly in positive or negative ways, and then separate. Nothing lasts, nothing is stable.

The more we cling to this unreal I and try to fulfil its demands, the deeper we bury ourselves in problems and confusion. Our classification of people into "friends," "enemies" and "strangers" is probably the best example of this.

We assume that the person we like has inherently good qualities and the person we dislike is inherently bad. We behave as though these qualities are permanent and unchanging; that we will always be close to the person we have labelled "friend" and never close to the person we dislike. And it is hard to imagine that an uninteresting person in the street could ever become a friend.

But these assumptions are mistaken, as our own experiences tell us. Relationships can and do change. The people we were once close to are now impossible to communicate with, and others whom we couldn't bear the sight of are now dear friends.

People change, our thoughts and feelings change, situations change. The changes that make us see a friend as an enemy can occur from one minute to the next, one year to the next, one lifetime to the next. The reasons for seeing someone as friend, enemy or stranger are not solid and incontrovertible. But holding onto them as if they were prevents us from seeing things as they really are and makes it difficult for us to deal with change when it occurs.

THE PRACTICE

Sit comfortably and generate the strong intention to do this meditation in order to develop perfect equanimity. Perhaps you would like to say some of the prayers on page 144.

Imagine in the space in front of you three people: someone you like, someone you dislike and someone you feel indifferent to. Retain the images of your friend, enemy and stranger throughout the meditation.

First, focus on your friend. Allow your feelings for him or her to arise. Feel your conviction that this person is definitely *friend,* that is, a person who is good to you and satisfies your needs. Feel how you really want this person to be happy. Immerse yourself in your good feelings.

Now, turn to your enemy, the person you do not like and who is not kind to you, who does not satisfy your needs; who annoys you and makes you angry; who hurts you. Look carefully at this man or woman; carefully note your feelings.

Finally, turn to the so-called stranger, this person you know a little but whom you neither like nor dislike. Look carefully at the person and note your feelings of indifference.

Now, recognize that the basis for your relationship to these three people is solely what they do or don't do for you, at this point in time. Is this a sound basis? Given the Buddhist view that our minds are beginningless, it follows that everyone has been our friend, enemy and stranger countless times before, so isn't it reasonable to be kind to your enemies now because they have been friends before?

Now, return to your friend and imagine a situation that would cause the relationship to end. Imagine your friend turning against you: feel the resentment and hurt, and how you no longer feel warm, no longer wish him or her well. Where is your friend now?

Recall that this person was not your friend before you were acquainted, and could very easily cease to be your friend now, as you have visualized.

Realize that there is no sound reason for feeling kind and loving towards only the friend of this moment. Relationships changed in the past and will continue to change. Today's friend can become tomorrow's enemy.

Now, turn to the present enemy. Imagine a situation in which you could be drawn together: a common interest, a word of praise or kindness. Look carefully at the person, and your feelings: are you softening? You *can* learn to feel warmly towards your enemy. This has happened before and will happen again. Why hold so strongly to the conception that this is definitely "enemy."

And what of the stranger? Imagine how one act of kindness or anger from this person could immediately turn him or her into a friend or enemy. There is no inherent, definite stranger there and no sound reason for your feelings of indifference. Remember that your present friend and enemy were stranger to you beforehand; this enemy could become friend or enemy now.

Keep the three people clearly in front of you. Think about the fragile impermanence of these relationships. It is only your misconceived belief in the stability of them that holds your mind back from the possibility of change.

Your friend, enemy and stranger all want happiness as much as you: in this respect everyone is equal. And everyone is equal in having the potential to develop their minds to the fullest and achieve ultimate clarity and compassion. The differences we see in people are superficial, based on our mistaken and narrow self-centred viewpoint. In fact, every-one is equal in deserving our care and compassion.

None of this means that we should not discriminate; on a practical level it is necessary. Naturally we feel closer to some people and are wise to keep our distance from others. This is not a contradiction. The point of the meditation is to develop equal concern, equal regard, for everyone, whether they help or harm us at this point in time; and to see that our present discrimination is based on arbitrary, mistaken and very changeable labels.

Finally, dedicate your positive energy and insight to the well-being and happiness of all.

7 *Meditation on Love*

Love is wanting others to be happy. It is a natural quality of mind, but until we develop it through meditation and other practices it remains limited, reserved for a few select individuals. Genuine love is universal in scope, extending to everyone, without exception.

Although we might agree with this idea in principle, we probably find it difficult to actualize. Does love arise spontaneously for all the people in the street and the supermarket? Do we feel love for the politicians we don't like, racists, and parents who beat their children? If not, we have work to do!

We should begin with mindfulness: observing our reactions to the people we encounter, looking out for feelings of attraction, aversion and indifference. As long as we continue to discriminate between those we like, those we dislike and those we do not care about we can never even take the first step.

To counteract this mistaken discrimination, we can practise the equilibrium meditation (page 89) and the methods for dealing with attachment and anger (page 97). The following meditation is a good complement to these; it helps us tap our natural resource of love and channel it to all living beings. If we practice it with concentration and sincerity, really getting in touch with our heart, we will find that it is possible to truly want others to be happy, regardless of their relationship to us.

THE PRACTICE

Sit comfortably. Relax your body and mind and let all thoughts and worries subside. Mindfully observe your breath until you are calm and your awareness is focussed in the here-and-now.

Start by imagining all living beings around you: your mother is on your left, your father on your right, and other relatives and friends are behind you. Visualize in front of you those you dislike or who have hurt you. And extending in every direction, right to the horizon, are all other beings. Feel that they are there, all in human form, sitting quietly, like you. Stay relaxed – don't feel crowded or tense, but imagine that a sense of harmony and peace pervades everyone.

Consider how nice it would be, for yourself and others, if you were able to love all these beings. Consider that everyone wants to be happy and to avoid suffering, just as you do. They are all trying to make the best of their lives, even those who are angry and violent.

Now generate a feeling of love in your heart. You can do this by thinking of someone you love and letting your natural good feelings for this person arise. You might like to imagine your love as a warm, bright light, not physical, but pure, positive energy glowing in your heart.

Before you can truly love others you need to love yourself. Loving yourself means accepting yourself as you are, with your present faults and shortcomings, and recognizing you have the potential to free yourself from all your problems. So, really wish yourself all the happiness and goodness there is. Imagine that the warm energy in your heart expands until it completely fills your body and mind.

Now let your love flow out to others. Start with your family and close friends sitting near you. Imagine the warm, luminous energy radiating from your body, touching them and filling their bodies and minds. Think, and feel sincerely,

"May you be happy; may all your thoughts be positive and all your experiences good. May you be free of problems, sickness and sadness. May your lives be long and peaceful and may you quickly reach enlightenment."

Then turn your attention to the people in front of you, those you have difficulty with. Contemplate that they also need and deserve your love. Imagine your positive, loving energy flowing out from your heart to these people. Wish them to be free of the confusion, the anger and self-centredness that drive them to act the way they do. Really want them to find peace of mind, happiness, and finally enlightenment. Pour out your love to all of them.

Continue to send your positive, warm feelings out to all the other people around you. Love is an unlimited spring of good energy, so you shouldn't worry that it will run out! Completely open your heart and imagine your love flowing to every direction, reaching all the beings who are lonely, sick, hungry, confused, oppressed, frustrated, frightened. Their suffering disappears and their minds become peaceful, clear and full of pure happiness. Wish them to have every good experience, from the satisfaction of ordinary needs and desires all the way to enlightenment. Concentrate on this feeling of love as long as possible.

Conclude the session by thinking that you definitely have the potential to love everyone, even those who annoy or hurt you, and those you don't even know. Generate a strong wish to work on your own anger, impatience, selfishness and the other problems that prevent you from having such love. Keeping your mind open and trying to overcome ego's prejudiced attitudes will leave much space in your heart for pure, universal love – and thus happiness for yourself and others – to develop.

Finally, dedicate the positive energy of your meditation to all beings, that they find happiness and enlightenment.

8   Dealing with Negative Energy

As mindfulness develops we become increasingly sensitive to our negative states of mind such as anger, irritation, pride, depression and so forth. Why are they considered "negative"? It is not that anger or desire are inherently evil or that we should feel ashamed when they arise. It is a matter of seeing them as the delusions that they are, distorted conceptions that paint a false picture of reality. They are negative because they lead to unhappiness and confusion.

Like all your experiences, negative emotions are impermanent, neither fixed nor concrete. They are simply mental energy, like love and joy, whose nature is clear and pure. Sometimes you might feel overwhelmed by them and doubt whether you can ever control your mind at all. But don't worry. Delusions come and go in your mind; they are not *you*. With proper understanding, every experience, whether positive or negative, can be a constructive step on the path.

Usually we either completely identify ourselves with our anger, for example, without any clarity or understanding at all, or suppress it altogether, refusing to recognize what is going on. Both approaches only make matters worse.

Instead, we can face our anger, analyze it to see how it is

mistaken, and apply counter-measures to bring our mind to a more realistic view of things. Dealing with anger or any other negative emotion in this way transforms it into a positive, learning experience.

We divide everything in the world outside us into *friend, enemy* and *stranger* (see page 89), according to our feelings towards them. Internally, all our feelings and attitudes can be divided into *attachment, aversion* and *ignorance*.

The root cause of negative emotions is the false notion of inherent, graspable, solid existence that we impute onto everything. This misconception branches into attachment, aversion and ignorance, which in turn branch out into all our other negative states of mind.

The methods explained in this chapter are practical ways of dealing with *attachment; anger,* perhaps the grossest expression of aversion; and *depression,* a dark, hopeless attitude that is rooted in ignorance, a kind of gross indifference. Most of the methods are simply ways of looking at these three states of mind. They are not magical solutions to what are, after all, difficult problems. Dealing with negative energy is hard work, but with practice and patience it is possible to gradually change our attitudes as a first step to changing our actual experience of people and situations.

Work with these methods in meditation; this makes it easier to apply them spontaneously when the need arises.

Attachment

To want something and not want to be separated from it: very broadly, this is attachment. Attendant to it is the false assumption that having whatever it is we want will bring satisfaction: this is why attachment causes problems.

Attachment is difficult to detect and even more difficult to find fault with; we think it is the road to happiness and satisfaction. But fulfilment of desire is an illusion; desire leads to more desire, not satisfaction.

We may be able to see how attachment to alcohol, drugs or money leads to problems rather than happiness, but we may wonder what is wrong with attachment to people. Wouldn't life be empty and meaningless without family and friends?

This question arises because we confuse attachment with love. Attachment is concerned with *my* needs, *my* happiness, while love is an unselfish attitude, concerned with the needs and happiness of others. Most of the time our love is mixed with attachment because we do not feel adequate or secure on our own, and try to find wholeness through another. But when a relationship involves attachment, problems inevitably arise. We become dependent on the good feelings and comfort of the relationship and then suffer when it changes. Real, lasting happiness can only be found within ourselves, and we will never find it as long as we lean helplessly on others. A relationship free of unrealistic grasping is free of disappointment, conflict, jealousy and other problems, and is fertile ground for the growth of love and wisdom.

Overcoming attachment does not mean becoming cold and indifferent. On the contrary, detachment means learning to have relaxed control over our mind through understanding the real causes of happiness and fulfilment, and this enables us to enjoy life more and suffer less.

Ways to deal with attachment

1. The best remedy is to think about emptiness (see page 58). Investigate the I that experiences the attachment. What is its nature? Try to locate this seemingly real, solid I in your body or mind.

Examine also the object of attachment. Is this person or thing inherently wonderful and pleasing? If so, why doesn't everyone appreciate it? Can you see how your mind exaggerates and gets excited about the object?

Try to see that both the I and its object are empty of inherent existence; they do not exist in the way they appear: in and of themselves. This might sound pretty unconvincing,

– especially when attachment is strong – but consider it carefully. Just thinking about emptiness is useful and helps us gradually to understand what it means, and to loosen the grasp of our attachment.

2. Meditate on death (see page 68). Remember the inevitability of death and that it could come at any time. Imagine how you will feel about separating forever from your objects of attachment: loved ones, enjoyments, possessions. Not only are they unable to help you as you die, but your attachment to them will upset your mind and hinder a peaceful death.

3. Contemplate the faults of attachment. Examine carefully the mind that experiences it. It is excited and full of unrealistic expectations. It glosses over the facts and deals with projected fantasies. It cannot see things clearly and is unable to make intelligent judgements. Is this happiness?

Also, the consequences of attachment are not peace and satisfaction, but disappointment and desire for more of the same. Think of the suffering you experience when you separate from an object of attachment. We all know the pain of relationships that did not work and the grief over a loved one's death.

Recognize that attachment is not a peaceful, clear state of mind, and that it leads to dissatifaction and unhappiness. And making a habit of it leaves on our mindstream imprints to experience more problems in the future.

Attachment clouds the mind and prevents us from recognizing its faults. It is very important to be honest with ourselves, to penetrate its facade and analyze its real nature.

4. Recall that all things are impermanent (see page 77). By their nature they change from moment to moment and will inevitably perish. The object of your attachment will not always be attractive and pleasing; visualize it as old, faded and worn and then check if your feelings about it remain the

same. And how would you feel if you lost it altogether?

The pleasure you experience is impermanent, too. For how long do you really feel pleased and satisfied with any one object?

When we recognize that external things cannot give us lasting happiness and satisfaction, our attachment to them will lessen – and we'll probably enjoy them all the more!

5. If you feel strongly attached to an attractive body (including your own), think about it in the following way.

First, analyze just what it is you find so attractive. Then mentally penetrate the surface and examine what lies beneath the skin: the flesh, bones, blood vessels and organs. Visualize the mucous, pus, blood, excrement and urine. Imagine it all in vivid detail. What is it you find so attractive here?

Imagine the body old, bent and wrinkled: where is the beautiful body now?

The point of this exercise is not to go to the other extreme and dislike yourself or the person you're attracted to. Rather it is to see how attachment distorts our perception and exaggerates the qualities of a person or thing. We simply don't see reality as it is. This analysis, therefore, brings us down to earth and helps us penetrate below the surface of our glossy fantasy image.

6. A remedy for attachment to food is to contemplate the suffering experienced by all the beings involved in its preparation. Animals are killed to provide us with meat and fish; innumerable small animals and insects are killed in the cultivation, fertilization and spraying of the grains, fruit and vegetables that we eat. Recall the hard work of the farmers, fishermen, fruitpickers, factory workers, truck drivers, shop assistants and cooks.

Try to eat mindfully, with appreciation for all these beings' kindness and sacrifice.

Anger

As opposed to attachment – wanting not to be separated from something or someone – anger is the attitude of wanting to be separated; of wanting to harm. Most of our anger is directed towards other people, but we can also be angry at ourselves or at inanimate objects. Anger ranges from a feeling of irritation about the way someone drinks tea, for example, to the powerful hatred that leads to physical violence or murder.

Anger is the very opposite of patience, tolerance and love. It is a distorted conception, a mistaken way of reacting to things, a delusion, and brings only problems and unhappiness, not the results we want. It disturbs our mind and causes us to hurt others through our actions and words, and is not an intelligent, skilful way to react, in any situation.

Patience, the opposite of anger, is a very valuable state of mind because it enables us to accept difficulties with a minimum of suffering. But patience has to be learned, and the way to develop it is by practising the remedies to anger.

The faults of anger are much easier to recognize than those of attachment; nevertheless, anger is very difficult to deal with. Part of the problem is our unwillingness even to admit that we have it, or, if we do recognize our anger, to admit that it is a fault. We may want to be peaceful and kind, but in our efforts we probably suppress feelings of dislike, annoyance and resentment, the more subtle aspects of anger. This is no solution. The emotions are still there, brewing below the surface of our mind, making us tense and nervous, and affecting other people.

Another mistaken approach is to see anger as a natural energy that should not be restrained but expressed whenever it arises. This may well relieve us of the immediate tension of our emotions and thus appear to be a skilful way of handling anger, but again it is no solution. We need only look at the short-term effects – how it disturbs ourselves and others – and the long-term – becoming habitually angry – to see that it is not at all useful or intelligent to give in to anger.

The truly skilful approach is to recognize the anger or irritation as it arises, keep it within our mind and deal with it there. Catching it when we first feel it is itself enough to defuse much of the anger-energy. Then we should examine the emotion from many angles: what are its causes? What do we hope to achieve by it? How do we view the situation? Having a clear understanding of anger gives us a firmer hold on it, because when we see how unreasonable it is, we are less likely to get involved in it.

Anger distorts our view of things. So, after examining it we should apply an antidote, such as one of the methods below, in order to bring our mind around to a more correct, realistic view. However, this is not easy. The energy of anger is very powerful, and we are not in the habit of trying to control or transform it. It is useful to use these methods over and over again in meditation, working with past experiences of anger or imagined situations; then, when anger occurs in our day-to-day relationships, we can bring to mind whatever insights we have developed in our practice sessions and try to avoid following the old familiar route of getting angry.

We won't always be successful, of course. Sometimes minutes, hours or days go by before we even realize that we got angry and hurt someone! But it is never too late to do something about it. Sit down, recall the situation, recognize what went wrong and figure out how to avoid the same mistakes again. We can also analyze in this way the problems we had years before. There is no reason to feel discouraged if anger continues to arise strongly; it takes time to break powerful habits. The important thing is to *want* and *try* to work on it.

Ways to deal with anger

1. When anger arises, turn your attention within and investigate the I that is angry. Analyze where and how it exists. Apply whatever understanding of emptiness you have.

Investigate the object of your anger also. Does it exist in the solid and definite way that it appears to you?

Try to see that the situation is like a dream: although it seems very real at the moment, from your point of view at a later time, even tomorrow, it will appear distant and faded, a mere memory.

2. Remember cause and effect. If someone harms you in some way – by being abusive or unfriendly, cheating or stealing from you, or wrecking your belongings – and it seems you have done nothing to deserve it, check again.

According to Buddhism, any misfortune that comes our way is the result of harmful actions we created in the past – in this or other lives. We reap what we have sown. When we can accept problems in this light, we simply won't feel the need to get angry.

3. Another method for dealing with people who hurt you is to put yourself in their place and try to see the situation from their point of view. What is driving them to behave in this way? Is their state of mind peaceful and happy, or confused, miserable and uncontrolled? They are human just like you, with problems and worries, trying to be happy and make the best of life. Recall your own experiences of being angry and unkind to get a better idea of what they are going through.

Also, consider that if they continue to be angry, what will the outcome be? Will they be happy and satisfied, or are they just creating more trouble and suffering for themselves? If we really understand others' confusion, we won't feel like react-ing with anger – why give them even more suffering?

4. Difficult situations are usually the most productive in terms of spiritual growth. Thus someone who arouses our anger is giving us a chance to learn that we still have work to do.

We might think we've come a long way in understanding and controlling our mind and that we are fairly peaceful now — but, all of a sudden, anger arises! It follows, then, that when people make us angry, they are giving us the chance to put our knowledge to use and increase our patience. Contemplate this and strengthen your determination to understand your anger, bring it under control and learn to react instead with patience. It will benefit yourself and others.

5. Contemplate the points of the death meditation. Death could happen at any time, so realize that it is ridiculous to cling to differences with people. Dying with unresolved anger creates havoc in your mind and makes a peaceful death impossible.

The other person could die at any time too. How would you feel if this happened before you were able to clear up the problems between you?

You, the other person and your interaction will definitely come to an end. Seen in this light, are the problems really so important? Are they worth the anguish and unhappiness they cause?

6. Having gained some control over your anger through one of these methods, you might like to work on developing love. You can do this by practising the meditation on love (page 94), visualizing in front of you the person who makes you angry and making a special effort to actually reverse your feelings for them.

7. All the methods explained above involve meditating to try to deal with anger on our own; it is also possible to resolve a conflict by communicating with the other person. But here we have to be careful. First of all we have to consider whether or not the other person would be open to such communication and if it would bring positive results. Secondly, we should check our motivation very carefully: do we really want to straighten out our differences with this person and come to a better mutual understanding, or do we just want to express how irritated we are or win a victory?

If we start discussing the problem with the desire to hurt or with expectations and demands, the communication will not work. So, we need to be very clear about our intentions and very sincere and honest in explaining our feelings. This kind of open communication is very powerful and can transform enemies into friends.

Of course, sometimes anger is very strong and the last thing you feel like doing is sitting down to meditate! At least you should try to avoid getting totally involved and speaking angrily or becoming violent. You can try some method for releasing your energy without harming the person, or become completely unresponsive, like stone or wood, until your anger has cooled down. Later, when your mind is more calm, you can meditate on the problem and apply one of the antidotes.

A frequently recurring problem, like getting angry at someone you live or work with, can be handled more effectively if you think about the situation in meditation and plan what to say and do when it next occurs. In that way, you are better prepared and less likely to be caught off-guard.

Depression

Depression is a dark, heavy, unhappy state of mind, self-centred and lacking in positive energy. It can be a chronic problem – a habitual response to difficulties – or the side-effect of an unfortunate experience, such as an illness or the death of a loved one. In any case, it is caused by the mistaken thinking that exaggerates the negative aspects of your personality or some situation and ignores the positive side.

Depression concentrates on *my* problem and blows it up out of proportion. Our thoughts spiral downwards; we feel the situation is hopeless with no possibility of improving. We feel sorry for ourselves, seeing our ego at the centre of a sad story, and we have little or no energy to share with others. Not only are we unable to take care of ourselves but we bring others down with us.

We all have the tendency to be depressed at times. We are not perfect, and life doesn't always go smoothly. We make mistakes, and we don't have control over what comes our way. When we are unable to accept these problems cheerfully as natural aspects of life or to deal with them skilfully, we become depressed. Of course, the pain we experience is real and the problems need to be taken care of. But sinking into depression is not the answer – it only deepens and complicates our unhappiness. The best solution is to analyze our thought patterns to see how we interpret the situation and try to recognize where we go wrong. Gradually we can learn to catch ourselves in time; to look at things more positively and to use our natural wisdom.

Ways to deal with depression

1. Investigate the I (see page 58), your sense of self that identifies strongly with unhappy thoughts and feelings. Try to find this I. What is its nature? Is is part of your body or your mind, or is it somewhere else? Is this depressed I something permanent, solid, unchanging?

Remember that your mind is a stream of different experiences – joyful, unhappy, positive, negative – all of the same clear, immaterial nature. These experiences appear and dissolve like waves on the ocean, lasting only a short time. Your depression is like a wave: a transient, ephemeral experience, so it is not appropriate to cling to it, thinking, "This is me."

2. Do the meditation on appreciating your human life (page 63). Even if your problem is a very serious one, it is important to remember that you have much positive energy and great potential. It is always possible to overcome depression by changing your way of thinking, by emphasizing the positive rather than the negative aspects of your personality and your life; they *do* exist! It's all a matter of you seeing and identifying with them rather than with your depressed low view of yourself.

3. Meditate on the clarity of your mind (page 47). Your unhappiness, worry and frustration, as well as your good

feelings, are all just mental energy – clear, non-material and transitory. Simply observe the different thoughts and experiences that pass through your mind, without judging them or getting involved in them.

4. Meditate on either love (page 94) or compassion (page 121). Turning outwards towards others and contemplating their needs and suffering will help you be less self-centred and thus see your problems more realistically.

5. Do one of the visualization meditations (page 109), for example, the body of light, Tara, or purification. These can be very fast ways to cut your depressed view of things.

Part Five
Visualization
Meditations

About Visualization

In your attempts to calm and concentrate your mind, you have probably noticed visual images among the many things that distract your attention from the object of meditation: faces of loved ones, your home, other familiar places, appetizing food, or memories of films you have seen. Such images arise spontaneously throughout the day but we are often too engrossed in external sensations to notice them. And each night our mind creates vivid scenes in which we interact with dream-people and dream-events. Visualization, or imagination, is thus a mental technique we are all familiar with, but unless our work lies in, say, art, design or film, we do little or nothing to develop and utilize it.

This natural capacity to think in pictures can be used to deepen our meditative experiences. Visualization is used in several ways in the Tibetan tradition of spiritual development. It adds another dimension to analytical meditations —for example, visualizing ourselves dying in order to sharpen the awareness of our mortality. A mental image of the Buddha is recommended as the focus of attention in the development of single-pointed concentration, and visualizing enlightened beings while praying helps to enhance our faith and conviction.

But the art of visualization is used to its optimum in Vajrayana, or tantra, the most profound and rapid means of reaching enlightenment. The practices of this path involve identifying oneself completely, body and mind, with an enlightened being and seeing one's environment as a pure realm. The ordinary, mistaken perceptions of oneself and all other phenomena are thus gradually abandoned as one's potential for enlightenment is allowed to express itself.

The meditational deities visualized in Vajrayana practice, such as Tara and Avalokiteshvara, are symbols of the enlightened state. Each is a manifestion of a specific quality – Avalokiteshvara, for example, is the buddha of compassion – but each also represents the total experience of enlightenment. The details of the visualization, such as colours, implements, hand gestures, posture and so forth, symbolize different aspects of the path to spiritual fulfilment.

Meditation on these deities (or images from other traditions that you are more comfortable with, for example, Christ or Mary) helps us to open our hearts to the pure energies of love, compassion, wisdom and strength that are ever-present, all around us, wherever we may be. And, as the potential for these enlightened qualities lies within us, we should consider the images we contemplate to be reflections of our own true nature. Although ultimate reality is inexpressible, words lead us to discover it; so too can images remind us of the experience of enlightenment until it becomes a living reality.

The two kinds of meditation – analytical and stabilizing – are used together in visualization techniques. We need analytical thought to construct the image at the beginning of the meditation and to recall it whenever it is lost during the session. Analysis is also used to deal with other problems that might occur, such as distraction or negative thoughts.

But developing a clear visualization depends primarily on

stabilizing meditation. Once the image has been established and we feel comfortable with it, we should hold it with single-pointed attention, not letting the mind be distracted to other objects. Initially, our concentration will last only a few seconds but with continual practice we will be able to maintain it for increasingly longer periods of time. Each time our attention wanders or we lose the object, we should again bring it to mind. This way of meditating both increases our familiarity with positive images and strengthens our ability to control and concentrate the mind.

It is common to find visualization difficult. If you are having problems, it could be that you are trying too hard or expecting too much. The mind needs to be in the right state – relaxed, clear and open. Too much effort creates tension, and the only vision that can appear is darkness. Too little concentration means the mind is crowded with distractions, leaving no space for a visualized image. We should learn to adjust our concentration as we would tune a musical instrument – with sensitivity and patience – until we have found the proper mental state in which the object can appear clearly.

Remember too that visualization utilizes only the *mental* faculty, not the eyes. If you find that you are straining to see something, you misunderstand the technique. Relax and let the image appear from within your mind.

Furthermore, we should be satisfied with whatever does appear, even if it is just a blur of colour or a minor detail. It is more important to have a sense or feeling of the presence of an enlightened being than be too concerned about seeing a mental image. Thus it is very important to be relaxed and free of expectations. It is self-defeating to expect a complete, perfect visualization after one or two attempts; it may take years of practice before you can really see the image. Again, it is a matter of tuning the mind to the right balance; learning to work with the energies and elements of the mind to produce a positive, joyful meditative experience.

You might find it useful to practise visualization with familiar objects. Sit quietly with your eyes closed and bring to mind the image of a friend, for example. Try to see the details: the colour and shape of the eyes, nose and mouth, the style of the hair, the shape of the body and so forth. Experiment with other objects: your house, the view from your window, even your own face.

Visualizing deities is made easier by gazing at a picture or statue, then closing your eyes and trying to recall the image in detail. However, this helps you with the details only; don't think your visualized figure should be flat like a drawing or cold and lifeless like a statue. It should be warm, full of life and feeling, three-dimensional and made of pure, radiant light. Feel that you are actually in the presence of a blissful, compassionate, enlightened being.

Finally, it might be useful to practise the following simple visualization before attempting more complicated techniques.

1   *Body of Light Meditation*

Sit comfortably, with your back straight, and breathe naturally. When your mind is calm and clear, visualize in the space above your head a sphere of white light, somewhat smaller than the size of your head, and pure, transparent and formless. Spend several minutes concentrating on the presence of the light. Don't worry if it does not appear sharply; it is enough just to feel it is there.

Contemplate that the sphere of light represents all universal goodness, love and wisdom: the fulfilment of your own highest potential. Then visualize that it decreases in size until it is about one inch in diameter and descends through the top of your head to your heart-centre. From there it begins to expand once more, slowly spreading to fill your entire body. As it does, all the solid parts of your body dissolve and become light – your organs, bones, blood vessels, tissue and skin all become pure, formless white light.

Concentrate on the experience of your body as a body of light. Think that all problems, negativities and hindrances have completely vanished, and that you have reached a state of wholeness and perfection. Feel serene and joyful. If any thought or distracting object should appear in your mind, let it also dissolve into white light. Meditate in this way for as long as you can.

2 *Purification Meditation*

There are both positive and negative aspects to our personality. On the one hand we have love, wisdom, joy and generosity, but on the other we have anger, selfishness, laziness and a long list of other problems. All these traits are just mental experiences, waves on the ocean of our consciousness; all have the same basic, clear nature. They are not static and permanent but constantly in flux, coming and going.

There are, however, two important distinctions to be made: positive states of mind are productive, beneficial for ourselves and others, whereas negative states are harmful and bring only confusion and pain. Peace of mind is achieved by cultivating what is positive and abandoning what is negative.

The second point is that anger and the other mental disorders arise from our misconceptions about the way things exist, while positive states of mind are realistic and arise from right understanding. When we recognize this and develop a correct view of reality, our negativities gradually lessen and eventually disappear altogether. As our wisdom develops, our spontaneous good feelings grow and our personality gradually transforms. At the end of this path is enlightenment, the perfection of all beneficial qualities – a state of great clarity and loving compassion.

Often we identify ourselves more with our negative side than our positive, and feel guilty about mistakes we have made. We believe, "I am hopeless; I can't control my anger; I don't do anything right; I'm completely cold and unable to love anyone." Although we may have faults and problems, it is wrong to think that they are permanent. We *can* free ourselves from negative energy and the burden of guilt, as long as we are willing to work. One way of doing this is through the process of purification.

Purification is a recurring theme in Buddhist meditation. It is chiefly a question of changing our way of thinking. When we think we are impure and negative, we become just that. A low, depressed self-image gradually permeates our behaviour and outlook on life. We feel limited and inadequate and don't even give ourselves a chance to change. But, by recognizing our potential for perfection and sincerely putting energy into developing it, we cultivate a more positive self-image. Believing that we are basically pure is the first step in becoming pure. What needs to be purified, therefore, is our lack of self-confidence and tendency to identify with our negative energy, as well as the negative energy itself.

This simplified meditation contains the essence of purification: letting go of problems and mistakes, seeing them as temporary obscurations, not as an intrinsic part of our nature. It helps us to get in touch with and develop our natural good energy.

THE PRACTICE

Be comfortable and relaxed. Take a few minutes to settle your mind in the here and now.

Then turn your attention to your breath. Breathe normally and observe the full duration of each inhalation and exhalation.

When you exhale, imagine that all your negative energy, past mistakes, distorted conceptions and emotions leave your body with the breath. Visualize this energy as black smoke and send it out into space, where it disappears completely. Feel confident that you have freed yourself from every trace of faults and negativity.

When you inhale, imagine that all the positive energy in the universe enters your body with the breath in the form of pure, radiant white light. Visualize this light flowing to every part of your body, filling every cell and atom, and making you relaxed, light and blissful.

Concentrate on this experience – breathing out the black smoke of your problems and breathing in the white light of good energy – for the duration of the session. When you are distracted by feelings, simply observe them without reacting or getting involved, transform them into the black smoke and breathe them out into oblivion.

Conclude the meditation by dedicating your positive energy to all beings finding everlasting happiness and peace of mind.

3   *Meditation on Tara*

Tara (the Liberator) is a buddha who represents in particular all enlightened beings' skilful activities, or the means by which they communicate with and guide us according to our ability. Contemplating Tara brings quick results in whatever we want and need. Known as the Mother of all Buddhas, she is our mother too, because she awakens and helps fulfil our potential to attain enlightenment.

THE PRACTICE

Relax your body and still your thoughts. Think that you will do this meditation for the benefit of all living beings.

Visualize in the space before you Tara, manifestation of all that is positive. Her body is of emerald-green light, translucent and radiant. (You can visualize her any size you like.)

Her left leg is drawn up, signifying complete control over sexual energy, and her right leg extended, indicating that she is ready to rise to the aid of all beings. Her left hand is at her heart in the refuge gesture: palm facing outward, thumb and ring finger touching, and the remaining three fingers raised.

Her right hand is on her right knee in the gesture of

granting sublime realizations: palm facing outward, thumb and first finger touching, the remaining fingers pointing down.

In each hand she holds the stem of a blue flower, symbol of the unblocking of the central channel (see page 134). She is exquisitely beautiful and smiles lovingly at you. Her clothing is of celestial silk and her ornaments of precious gems.

Concentrate for some time on the visualization, opening your heart to the energy of Tara's inexhaustible loving-kindness.

Next, think of your problems, your needs and aims, and make a prayer to Tara from your heart, asking her for help. She responds at once by sending streams of light into you: white light flows from her forehead into yours, eliminating all obstacles and negativities of body; red light flows from her throat into yours, eliminating all obstacles and negativities of speech; and blue light flows from her heart into yours, eliminating all obstacles and negativities of mind. Visualize each of these in turn; really feel that you are now completely free of all problems and that you have received the inspiration and energy to accomplish your objectives.

Then, Tara comes to the space above your head, facing the same way as you. She dissolves into green light, which descends through the crown of your head to your heart-centre, the seat of your consciousness. Your mind merges indistinguishably with Tara's mind and you experience clarity, tranquillity and bliss.

Remain in this state as long as possible. When thoughts arise, simply observe them with detachment, judging them neither good nor bad, and return your attention to the experience of clarity and bliss.

At the end of the session, dedicate the positive energy you generated to all living beings, that they might attain the great joy of liberation from confusion and suffering. (For another meditation on Tara and her mantra, see page 171.)

4   Meditation on Compassion

Whereas love is the desire for others to be happy, compassion is the desire actually to bring about their happiness by freeing them from their suffering.

Compassion is not the sad, anxious feeling we often experience when we see or hear about people's pain. Neither is it a sentimental involvement in their problems nor, on the other hand, a self-conscious holding-back. All these responses are inappropriate and show that we do not understand the causes of the problems, or the solution.

With true compassion we are more wise: we understand how and why suffering occurs and can deal realistically with the situation. It gives us the energy to do what we can to help and the wisdom to accept our limitations and not worry about what we cannot do.

An *attitude* of compassion is what really counts; we cannot expect to actually eliminate someone else's unhappiness while our own mind is still troubled by misconceptions and confused emotions. We should, therefore, work simultaneously on developing the wisdom to see clearly how things are and the compassionate wish to alleviate others' suffering – then our actions will be truly skilful.

Compassion benefiits not only others but ourselves as well. As the Dalai Lama has said, "If you want others to be happy, practise loving-compassion; if you want yourself to be happy, practise loving-compassion."

We all possess the potential to be limitlessly compassionate. A powerful way of awakening and developing this potential is by visualizing Avalokiteshvara (Tibetan: Chenrezig), the embodiment of compassion, and contemplating his mantra.

A mantra is a series of syllables that corresponds to certain subtle vibrations within us. A mantra has built up its energy for good by being used by millions of people for thousands of years. Its effectiveness does not lie in our understanding its literal meaning but in concentrating on its sound as we recite it aloud or silently.

Avalokiteshvara's mantra, *om mani padme hum* (pronounced *om mah-nee ped-may hoom*), expresses the pure energy of compassion that exists in every being. Reciting it, either in meditation or while going about our daily activities, not only awakens our own compassion but, by joining with the millions of other people saying it too, adds to the growth of peaceful, loving energy in the world. At the very least, concentrating on the compassion-mantra helps our mind stay alert and positive rather than scattered and negative.

This practice combines an analytical meditation for generating compassion with a stablizing meditation on the image and mantra of Avalokiteshvara.

THE PRACTICE

Relax your body and mind and bring your awareness to the present by mindfully watching your breath. Check your thoughts and feelings and generate a positive motivation for doing the meditation.

Imagine that all of space is filled with beings, sitting around you and extending beyond the horizon. Contemplate their suffering. First, think of the suffering of your parents and the other people you are close to. Open your heart to the

physical and psychological problems they are experiencing and think that, just like you, they want to be free of all suffering. Feel how wonderful it would be if they *were* free and could enjoy the peace and bliss of enlightenment.

Then think of the people you do not like or who have hurt you. Imagine their suffering: physical pain and discomfort, feelings of loneliness, insecurity, fear, dissatisfaction. Just like you, they don't want problems but they have no choice: as long as the mind is confused and ignorant of reality, it cannot find peace. Open your heart to these people for whom normally you feel irritation or anger.

Expand your awareness to take in the troubles and pain of other human beings and of animals; whoever has an uncontrolled mind necessarily has suffering.

But don't be overwhelmed by all of this! Remember that suffering, unhappiness and pain are mental experiences, impermanent and changeable. They arise because of misunderstanding and confused emotions, and once their causes have been eliminated they disappear. It is a matter of each one of us working on our own mind, dealing with our misconceptions and negative energy and gradually developing a correct understanding of the way things actually exist.

Feel strongly the aspiration to do this yourself, so that you can help others to be free of their suffering.

Now, visualize just above your head and facing the same way as you Avalokiteshvara, the manifestation of pure unobstructed compassion, love and wisdom. His body is of white light, transparent and radiant. Try to feel his living presence.

His face is peaceful and smiling and he radiates his love to you and all the beings surrounding you. He has four arms. His first two hands are together at his heart and hold a jewel that fulfils all wishes; his second two are raised to the level of his shoulders, the right holding a crystal rosary and the left a white lotus. He is sitting on a white moon disc upon an open lotus, his legs crossed in the full-lotus posture. He wears exquisite silk and precious jewels.

Hold your awareness on this visualization until it is stable. Stay relaxed and comfortable and open to Avalokiteshvara's serene and loving energy.

Now, make a prayer from your heart, to overcome your misconceptions and negative energy and to develop pure love and compassion for all beings. Feel that you are connecting with your own true nature, your highest potential.

In response to your request, Avalokiteshvara lovingly sends streams of white light, filling every cell and atom of your body. It purifies all your negativities and problems, all your past harmful actions and your potential to give harm in the future, and completely fills you with his limitless love and compassion. Your body feels light and blissful, your mind peaceful and clear.

The light from Avalokiteshvara radiates out to every living being, purifying their negative energy and filling them with bliss.

Now, while concentrating on this visualization, recite the mantra, *om mani padme hum,* aloud for a while and then silently, as many times as you like.

When you have finished the recitation, visualize Avalokiteshvara dissolving into white light, which flows down through the crown of your head and reaches your heart-centre. Your mind merges indistinguishably with Avalokiteshvara's mind and you experience complete tranquillity and bliss.

Hold this feeling as long as possible. Whenever your usual sense of I starts to arise – an I that is bored, restless, hungry; whatever – think that this is not your real self. Simply bring your attention back again and again to the experience of being oneness with the qualities of Avalokiteshvara's mind: infinite love and compassion.

Finally, dedicate the positive energy you have created by doing this meditation to the happiness of all living beings. (For another meditation on Avalokiteshvara, see page 160.)

5   *Meditation on the Buddha*

"Buddha" is a Sanskrit word that means "fully awakened." It refers not only to Shakyamuni, or Gautama, the founder of the teachings that came to be known as Buddhism, but also to any person who attains enlightenment. There are numberless enlightened beings – beings who have completely transformed their minds, eliminated all negative energy and become whole, perfect. They are not confined to a transient, physical body as we are, but are free from death and rebirth. They can abide in a state of pure consciousness, or appear in different forms – a sunset, music, a beggar, a teacher – in order to communicate their wisdom and love to ordinary beings. They are the very essence of compassion and wisdom, and their energy is all around us, all the time.

Every living being, by virtue of having a mind, is able to become a buddha. The fundamental nature of the mind is pure, clear and free of the clouds of disturbing conceptions and emotions that now obscure it. As long as we identify with confused states of mind, believing, "I am an angry person; I am depressed; I have so many problems," we don't even give ourselves the chance to change.

Of course, our problems *are* very deep and complex, but they are not as real or as solid as we think. We also have the wisdom that can recognize our mistaken thinking, and the capacity to give and to love. It is a matter of identifying with and gradually developing *these* qualities to the point where they arise spontaneously and effortlessly. It is not easy to become enlightened, but it is possible.

In this meditation, we visualize the form of Shakyamuni Buddha and recite his mantra.

Shakyamuni was born a prince, Siddhartha, into a vastly wealthy family two-and-a-half thousand years ago in the north of India. He lived in his kingdom for twenty-nine years, sheltered from the more unpleasant realities of human existence. He eventually encountered them however in the form of a sick person, an old, senile person and a corpse. These experiences affected him profoundly. His next significant encounter was with a wandering meditator who had transcended the concerns of ordinary life and reached a state of balance and serenity.

Realizing that his way of life led only to death and had no real, lasting value, Prince Siddhartha decided to leave his home and family and go to the forest to meditate. After many years of persistent, single-minded effort, meeting and overcoming one difficulty after another, he attained enlightenment – became a buddha. Having thus freed himself from all delusions and suffering, he aspired to help others reach enlightenment too; his compassion was limitless.

He was now thirty-five years old. He spent the remaining forty-five years of his life explaining the way to understand the mind, deal with problems, develop love and compassion and thus become enlightened. His teachings were remarkably fluid, varying according to the needs, capabilities and personalities of his listeners. He led them skilfully towards the understanding of the ultimate nature of reality.

The Buddha's life itself was a teaching, an example of the path to enlightenment, and his death a teaching on impermanence.

A powerful way to discover our own buddha-nature is to open ourselves to the external buddha. With continual practice, our ordinary self-image gradually falls away and we learn instead to identify with our innate wisdom and compassion: our own buddhahood.

THE PRACTICE

Calm your mind by doing a few moments of breathing meditation. Then, contemplate the prayer of refuge and bodhicitta.

> I take refuge until I am enlightened,
> In the buddhas, the dharma and the sangha.
> Through the merit I create by practising giving
>   and the other perfections,
> May I attain buddhahood for the sake of
>   all living beings.

Generate love and compassion by reflecting briefly on the predicament of all beings: their wish to experience true happiness but inability to obtain it, and their wish to avoid suffering but continual encounters with it.

Then think: "In order to help all beings and lead them to the perfect peace and happiness of enlightenment I myself must attain enlightenment. For this purpose I shall practise this meditation."

Visualization of the Buddha: Every aspect of the visualization is of light: transparent, intangible and radiant. At the level of your forehead and between six and eight feet away is a large golden throne adorned with jewels and supported at each of its four corners by a pair of snow lions. These animals, in reality manifestations of bodhisattvas, have white fur and a green mane and tail.

On the flat surface of the throne is a seat consisting of a large open lotus and two radiant discs representing the sun and the moon, one on top of the other. These three objects symbolize the three principal realizations of the path to enlightenment: the lotus, renunciation; the sun, emptiness; and the moon, bodhicitta.

Seated upon this is the Buddha, who has attained these realizations and is the embodiment of all enlightened beings. His body is of golden light and he wears the saffron robes of a monk. His robes do not actually touch his body but are separated from it by about an inch. He is seated in the vajra, or full–lotus, posture. The palm of his right hand rests on his right knee, the fingers touching the moon cushion, signifying his great control. His left hand rests in his lap in the meditation pose, holding a bowl filled with nectar, which is medicine for curing our disturbing states of mind and other hindrances.

Buddha's face is very beautiful. His smiling, compassionate gaze is directed at you and, simultaneously, towards every other living being. Feel that he is free of all judging, critical thoughts and that he accepts you just as you are. His eyes are long and narrow. His lips are cherry red and the lobes of his ears are long. His hair is blue-black and each hair is individually curled to the right and not mixed with the others. Every feature of his appearance represents an attribute of his omniscient mind.

Rays of light emanate from each pore of Buddha's pure body and reach every corner of the universe. These rays are actually composed of countless miniature buddhas, some going out to help living beings, others dissolving back into his body, having finished their work.

Purification: Feel the living presence of Buddha and take refuge in him, recalling his perfect qualities and his willingness and ability to help you. Make a request from your heart to receive his blessings to help you to become free from all your negative energy, misconceptions and other problems and to receive all the realizations of the path to enlightenment.

Your request is accepted. A stream of purifying white light, which is in the nature of the enlightened mind, flows from Buddha's heart and enters your body through the crown of your head. Just as the darkness in a room is instantly dispelled the moment a light is switched on, so too is the darkness of your negative energy dispelled upon contact with this radiant white light.

As it flows into you, filling your body completely, recite the following prayer three times.

> To the guru and founder,
> The endowed transcendent destroyer,
> The one-thus-gone, the foe destroyer,
> The completely perfected, fully-awakened being,
> The glorious conqueror, the subduer from the
>   Shakya clan,
> I prostrate, turn for refuge and make offerings:
> Please bestow your blessings.

Now, recite Buddha's mantra, *Tayata om muni muni maha munaye soha* (pronounced *ta-ya-ta om mooni mooni ma-ha moon-aye-ye so-ha*). Repeat it out loud, or chant it, at least seven times, then say it quietly to yourself for a few minutes.

When you have finished reciting, feel that all your negative energy, problems and subtle obscurations have been completely purified. Your body feels blissful and light. Concentrate on this for a while.

Receiving inspiring strength: Visualize that a stream of golden light descends from the Buddha's heart and flows into your body through the crown of your head. The essence of this light is the excellent qualities of his pure body, speech and mind.

He can transform his body into different forms, animate and inanimate, to help living beings according to their individual needs and particular states of mind.

With his speech he can communicate different aspects of the dharma simultaneously to beings of various levels of development and be understood by them in their respective languages.

His omniscient mind sees clearly every atom of existence and every occurrence – past, present and future – and knows the thoughts of every living being: such is his awareness in each moment.

These infinite good qualities flow into every part of your body. Concentrate on this blissful experience while again repeating the mantra, *tayata om muni muni maha munaye soha.*

When you have finished the recitation feel that you have received the infinite excellent qualities of Buddha's body, speech and mind. Your body feels light and blissful. Concentrate on this for some time.

Absorption of the visualization: Now, visualize that the eight snow lions absorb into the throne, the throne into the lotus and the lotus into the sun and moon. They, in turn, absorb into the Buddha, who now comes to the space above your head, melts into light and dissolves into your body.

Your ordinary sense of I – unworthy and burdened with faults – and all your other wrong conceptions disappear completely. In that instant you become one with the Buddha's blissful, omniscient mind in the aspect of vast empty space.

Concentrate on this experience for as long as possible, allowing no other thoughts to distract you.

Then, imagine that from this empty state there appear in the place where you are sitting the throne, lotus, sun, moon and upon these yourself as the Buddha. Everything is of the nature of light, exactly as you had visualized before in front of you. Feel that you *are* Buddha. Identify with his enlightened wisdom and compassion instead of with your usual incorrect self-view.

Surrounding you in every direction and filling all of space are all living beings. Generate love and compassion for them by recalling that they too want to achieve happiness and peace of mind and freedom from all problems. Now that you are enlightened you can help them.

At your heart are a lotus and a moon. Standing upright around the circumference of the moon, reading clockwise, are the syllables of the mantra, *tayata om muni muni maha munaye soha*. The seed-syllable *mum (moom)* stands at the moon's centre.

Visualize that rays of light – actually your wisdom and compassion – emanate from each letter and spread in all directions. They reach the countless sentient beings surrounding you and completely purify them of their obscurations and delusions and fill them with inspiration and strength.

While imagining this, again recite the mantra, *tayata om muni muni maha munaye soha*.

When you have finished reciting, think: "Now I have led all sentient beings to enlightenment, thus fulfilling my intention for doing this meditation."

Visualize that everyone surrounding you is now in the form of Buddha and is experiencing complete bliss and the wisdom of emptiness.

You should not worry that your meditation is a sham and that you have not helped even one person achieve enlightenment. This practice is known as "bringing the future result into the present path" and is a powerful cause for our own enlightenment. It helps us develop firm conviction in our innate perfection – our buddha-potential; that what we have just done in meditation we will definitely accomplish one day.

Conclude the session by dedicating all the positive energy and insight you have gained by doing this meditation to your eventual attainment of enlightenment for the benefit of all living beings.

6   *Inner Heat Meditation*

This meditation is an especially powerful Vajrayana method for tapping and skilfully utilizing our innate blissful mental energy.

There is an intimate relationship between our mind and subtle nervous system. Mental energy flows through the body within a psychic nervous system composed of thousands of thin, transparent, subtle channels. The principal ones – known as the central, right and left channels – run parallel to and just in front of the spinal column. Pure mental energy can function only within the central channel, whereas deluded energy flows through all the others.

At present, our central channel is blocked by knots of negative energy – anger, jealousy, desire, pride and so forth – at points (*chakras*) corresponding to the base of the spine, navel, heart, throat and crown. To the extent that this deluded energy is active, the pure energy of mind is blocked and unable to function. Recall, for example, the enormous physical and mental tension created by strong desire or anger; there is no space at all for calmness and clarity.

The inner heat meditation is an excellent method for transforming this powerful energy and developing spontaneous control over all our actions of body, speech and mind. Mere suppression of attachment, anger and other emotions does not eliminate them; it compounds them. The solution is literally to transform this energy – which by its nature is neither good nor bad – into blissful, free-flowing energy.

Skilful practice of the meditation will show us that we are capable of happiness and satisfaction without needing to rely upon external objects – an idea that is inconceivable for most of us.

This practice also helps us in our development of single-pointed concentration. Normally, our dissatisfied mind wanders uncontrollably, blown here and there by the force of deluded energy in the psychic channels; yet if we could have an experience of bliss pleasurable enough to concentrate on, we simply would not *want* to wander elsewhere.

THE PRACTICE

Sit comfortably in your meditation place and generate a strong positive motivation for doing this inner heat practice. Determine to keep your mind relaxed, concentrated and free of expectations for the entire session.

Start by visualizing the central channel as a transparent, hollow tube, a finger's breadth in diameter. It runs straight down through the centre of the body, just in front of the spinal column, from the crown of your head to the base of your spine.

Next, visualize the right and left lateral channels, slightly thinner than the central one. They start from the right and left nostrils respectively, travel upwards to the top of the head and then curve over to run downwards on either side of the central channel. They curve inwards and join the central channel at a point approximately four fingers' breadth below the level of the navel.

Take as long as you like to construct this visualization. Once it is stable, imagine a red-hot ember the size of a tiny seed inside the central channel at the level of the navel. To strengthen this visualization, imagine reaching into a fire, taking out a tiny glowing ember and placing it in your central channel. Once it is there, really feel its intense heat.

Now, in order to increase the heat, gently contract the muscles of the pelvic floor, concentrating on the internal rather than the external muscles, and in this way bring air energy up from the lowest chakra to the ember.

Next, gently take a full breath through both nostrils. The air travels from the nostrils down through the right and left channels to where they enter the central channel just below the level of the navel. The air joins with the heat there and with the energy brought up from below.

As you stop inhaling, immediately swallow and push down gently with your diaphragm in order to firmly compress the energy brought down from above: now the air energy is completely locked in, compressed from above and below.

Now, hold your breath as long as it is comfortable to do so. Concentrate completely on the ember in the navel area, whose heat is increasing and spreading as a result of the compressed air energy.

When you are ready, relax your lightly tensed muscles and exhale gently and completely. Although the air leaves through the nostrils, visualize that it rises up through the central channel and dissolves there. The heat emanating from the burning ember at the navel continually increases and spreads and starts to burn away the blockages at each chakra and starts also to warm the concentration of silvery blissful energy found at the crown chakra.

However, the focal point of your concentration is always the heat of the burning ember in the navel area.

Once your first exhalation is complete, again tighten the lower muscles, inhale a second time, swallow and push down with the diaphragm, thus again compressing the air and intensifying the heat. Hold your breath and concentrate on the heat, then exhale, releasing the air up the central channel once again.

Repeat the entire cycle rhythmically seven times altogether, the intensity of the heat growing with each breath.

At the seventh exhalation, imagine that the now burning-hot ember explodes into flames. They shoot up the central channel, completely consuming and purifying the deluded energy at each chakra. At the crown, the flames finally melt and release the silvery blissful energy, which pours down the purified central channel giving increasing pleasure at each chakra it passes. Finally, when it meets the blazing ember at the navel chakra, there is an explosion of bliss. This blissful heat flows out to every atom and cell of your body, completely filling you, making your mind very happy.

Concentrate on this pleasure without tension or expectation; without clinging to it or analyzing it. Just relax and enjoy it.

You will notice that, no matter how strong the pleasure is, your mind and body are calm and controlled, unlike our usual experiences of physical pleasure when the mind is excited and uncontrolled.

If your mind should wander from its concentration to other objects – the past or future, objects of attachment or aversion – focus your attention on the *subject* of the thought, the mind that perceives the distracting object, the thinker. Watch the subject until the distracting thought disappears, then concentrate again on the blissful feeling.

Analysis of feeling: Having reached a state of clarity, it is good to use it to discover the nature of your mind. After concentrating on your feeling, being absorbed in it for some time, analyze it by contemplating each of the following questions. Take as long as you like.

Is the feeling permanent or impermanent? How? Why?

Is the feeling blissful or suffering? How? Why?

Is the feeling related or unrelated to the nervous system and the mind? How? Why?

Does the feeling exist inherently, from its own side, without depending on anything else, or not? How? Why?

Examine each point from every angle. Finish the session by summing up your conclusion, then dedicate any positive energy and insight gained during the meditation to your speedy enlightenment for the sake of all living beings.

Part Six
Devotional
Practices

About Devotion

The idea of devotion makes some people uneasy because they equate it with blind faith and mindless submissiveness. But proper devotion is not like that. It is, in fact, a very positive attitude: to be devoted to one's family, friends or work is to have love, care and responsibility. In this sense it means going beyond our usual narrow, self-centred thoughts and concerns, and dedicating our energy to others.

Of course, if our devotion is not well-founded or its object is unreliable, we will only be disappointed and feel doubt and resentment. But if it is based on clear, correct understanding and its object is one that will not let us down, the experience will be rich and productive.

In Buddhism, devotion is associated with *refuge,* the first step on the path to liberation and awakening. Refuge is the attitude of relying upon, or turning to, something for guidance and help. In an ordinary sense we take refuge in friends for love and security, in food and entertainment when we are hungry and bored, and so forth. But such external sources of refuge can satisfy our needs only temporarily because they, as well as the happiness they bring, are impermanent and unreliable.

Buddhist refuge, on the other hand, involves discovering and utilizing the unlimited potential that lies within each of us. There are two aspects of refuge, outer and inner. Outer refuge is appreciating and relying upon the *three jewels: buddha, dharma* and *sangha*. *Buddha* refers both to the enlightened state itself – the removal of all negative qualities and the perfection of all positive – and to those who have attained enlightenment. Refuge in buddha means opening our heart to the love and wisdom offered by these beings and accepting their guidance on the spiritual path.

Dharma refers to wisdom, the realizations that comprise the progressive stages of the path to enlightenment. The literal meaning of the Sanskrit term *dharma* is "to hold" – it includes any method that holds or protects us from problems. Buddha's teachings are known as dharma because they come from his actual experience of eliminating every trace of confusion and negative energy from his mind. Refuge in dharma means practising the prescribed methods, aspiring to awaken within ourselves the wisdom that every enlightened being has discovered.

Sangha refers to the spiritual community, those who have wisdom and give us inspiration and support. Buddha and dharma provide us with the basis of our practice but sangha provide the help we need to make the practice actually work. Talking with like-minded friends, for example, can give us answers to questions and solutions to problems; meditating together gives us strength and encouragement; a community of meditators offers a peaceful haven from the craziness of city life. Refuge in sangha means respecting such friends and accepting their help.

Inner refuge is refuge in ourselves, in our ultimate potential. The three refuge objects have their internal counterparts: the inner buddha is the seed of enlightenment that lies in the mind of each sentient being, without exception; the inner dharma is our natural wisdom that can distinguish real from false; the inner sangha is the guidance and inspiration that we can give others. As human beings, we have the potential to develop unlimited love, compassion and wisdom and to free ourselves from all negative energy – in other words, to reach the same level as a buddha.

Usually we find it difficult to feel good about ourselves and to have confidence in our own potential – instead we take refuge in outside things. Just imagine the boredom, the uneasiness and the games the mind would play if we were completely alone for a day, or even an hour, cut off from people, books, television and all external means of occupying ourselves! We can't conceive of living without sense objects – the external world. However, it *is* possible to be completely satisfied and happy, whatever the situation, by relying solely on our inner resources. The external refuge objects exist to awaken us to these resources, to our inner buddha, dharma and sangha. When we recognize and nourish this potential, we have found the real meaning of refuge.

Refuge is a fundamental step on this spiritual path, and devotion is an essential component of it. It should not be an ignorant, emotional attitude, but one that is sound and intelligent, based on clear understanding of what buddha, dharma and sangha really are and what they can do for us. We *do* need help to travel the path to inner awakening, but we need to check carefully the qualifications of the teachers we meet and the effectiveness of their methods, not just follow the advice of anyone with a nice vibration or a charismatic personality. It's a question of getting to know a teacher or a path, examining, reflecting, experimenting, being honest and sincere. All this may take some time, but it is very important to make sure that any devotion we do cultivate will be appropriate and productive, not a waste of energy.

The practices presented in this section are called "devotional" because they involve a certain commitment to the Buddhist path. If you don't feel such a commitment, you can simply read through this section, or experiment with the methods if you like.

The purpose and psychological effects of each practice are explained here as clearly as possible, but the real taste comes only by doing them, with understanding and devotion.

1   *Prayers*

The success of any project – climbing a mountain, writing a book or baking a cake – hinges on the care we take in the preparatory work. The same is true for meditation. A successful meditation session depends primarily on our state of mind, and the appropriate inner state can be induced through reciting certain prayers, verbally or mentally, with understanding and sincerity.

Prayer is not the mechanical repetition of words but an opening of the heart to communicate with our true nature. The words serve us as a reminder of what we are trying to achieve, and actually help create the cause for whatever we are praying for to occur in the future.

(See the Appendix for the phonetics of these prayers in Tibetan)

PRAYERS TO BE SAID AT THE START OF A MEDITATION SESSION

1   *Prayer of refuge and bodhicitta*

> I take refuge until I am enlightened
> In the buddhas, the dharma and the sangha.
> Through the merit I create by practising giving and the
>   other perfections
> May I attain buddhahood for the sake of all sentient
>   beings. (3 times)

2 *The four immeasurable thoughts*

May all sentient beings have happiness and the causes
   of happiness;
May all sentient beings be free from suffering and the
   causes of suffering;
May all sentient beings never be separated from the
   happiness that knows no suffering;
May all sentient beings abide in equanimity, free
   from attachment and anger that hold some close and
   others distant.

3 *Refuge in the guru*

The guru is buddha, the guru is dharma,
The guru is sangha, also;
The guru is the creator of all happiness:
In all gurus I take refuge. (3 times)

4 *The seven limbs*

Reverently I prostrate with my body, speech and mind
And present clouds of every type of offering, actual
   and mentally transformed.
I declare all my negative actions accumulated since
   beginningless time
And rejoice in the merit of all holy and ordinary
   beings.
Please remain until samsara ends
And turn the wheel of dharma for sentient beings.
I dedicate the merit created by myself and others to
   the great enlightenment.

5 *Mandala offering*

Om indestructible base *ah hum!*
Mighty golden base.
Om indestructible wall *ah hum!*
Outside, a surrounding wall encircles it.
In the centre, the king of mountains, Mt. Meru.

East: the continent Noble Body.
South: Jambu-fruit-land.
West: Cattle Enjoyments.
North: Unpleasant Voice.
The subcontinents of Noble-body-land.
Yak-tail and Other Yak-tail Islands.
Moving and Travelling the Highest Path (Islands).
Unpleasant Voice and Moon of Unpleasant Voice (Islands).
In the east the treasure mountain,
In the south the wish-granting tree,
In the west the wish-granting cow,
In the north the uncultivated crops.
The precious wheel,
The precious jewel,
The precious queen,
The precious minister,
The precious elephant,
The precious supreme horse,
The precious general,
The great treasure vase.
The goddess of grace,
Goddess of garlands,
Goddess of song,
Goddess of dance,
Goddess of flowers,
Goddess of incense,
Goddess of light,
Goddess of perfume.
The sun, the moon,
The umbrella of all precious things,
The banner of victory in every direction,
And in the centre,
All the possessions precious to gods and humans.
This magnificent and glorious collection,
Lacking in nothing,
I offer to you, root and lineage Gurus,
Especially to Buddha Shakyamuni,

Together with the entire assembly of deities.
For the welfare of sentient beings,
Please accept these offerings through your compassion,
And thus may I and all beings in space
Receive blessings.

Short outer mandala

The fundamental ground is scented with incense and
 strewn with flowers,
Adorned with Mount Meru, the four continents, the sun
 and the moon.
I imagine this as a buddha-land and offer it.
May all living beings enjoy this pure realm.

Inner mandala

The objects of my attachment, aversion and ignorance
 —friends, enemies and strangers—
My body, wealth and enjoyments;
Without any sense of loss I offer this collection.
Please accept it with pleasure
And bless me with freedom from the three poisons.

I send forth this jewelled mandala to you precious gurus.

PRAYERS TO BE SAID AT THE CONCLUSION OF
A MEDITATION SESSION

6 *Dedication of merit*

Through this virtuous action
May I quickly attain the state of a guru-buddha
And lead every living being, without exception,
Into that pure world.

7 *Bodhicitta prayer*

May the supreme jewel bodhicitta
That has not arisen, arise and grow;
And may that which has arisen not diminish
But increase more and more.

2   Explanation of the prayers

1 *Prayer of refuge and bodhicitta*

This prayer expresses the most positive, beneficial intention we could have for engaging in study or meditation on the path to enlightenment.

The first part of the prayer deals with *refuge*, the attitude of turning to the buddha, dharma and sangha for guidance and help (see page 141). Remember the two aspects of refuge, outer and inner, and feel confident that the seed of enlightenment lies within your own mind.

The second part of the prayer is the generation of *bodhicitta*, the mind set on enlightenment. Bodhicitta, founded on pure love and compassion for every living being, is the dedicated determination to become a buddha solely to help others achieve enlightenment too.

The path of an enlightenment-bound person – a bodhisattva – involves the development of the *six perfections* (Sanskrit: *paramita*): giving, moral discipline, patience, joyous effort, concentration and wisdom. These six, practised with the motive of helping others achieve enlightenment, provide nourishment for the seed of enlightenment to grow in our own mind. The gradual development of each perfection progressively erodes our delusions, making space for the wisdom that understands reality.

Anything we do – meditation, eating, sleeping or working – automatically becomes a cause for enlightenment if it is done with the thought of bodhicitta.

Refuge and bodhicitta give life and meaning to our meditations. You can recite the prayer three times before each session, and it is best if you can also visualize the Buddha in front of you (see page 126), seeing him as the embodiment of the qualities you are trying to develop within yourself.

2 *The four immeasurable thoughts*

The four thoughts expressed in this prayer are called immeasurable because they extend to all beings throughout the infinite universe. The first is *immeasurable love*: the desire for all beings to be happy. The second is *immeasurable compassion*: the desire for all beings to be free of suffering. The third is *immeasurable joy:* the desire for all beings to experience the ultimate happiness that lasts forever. The fourth is *immeasurable equanimity*: the desire for all beings to be free of the attachment and aversion that cause us to distinguish between friend, enemy and stranger.

Each line of the prayer is a meditation in itself and its heartfelt recitation creates the cause for our development of universal awareness and concern for others.

3 *Refuge in the guru*

There are countless beings who have reached enlightenment, and these buddhas actively help all sentient beings. The most effective way they help is by instructing us in the knowledge and techniques of the path to enlightenment. Because of our obscurations we are unable to perceive enlightened beings directly, so they reach us through spiritual teachers (Sanskrit: *guru*; Tibetan: *lama*). By recognizing our teachers as one with the buddhas, we are able to make direct contact with the enlightened state and and eventually to actualize it ourselves. This practice, known as guru-yoga, is the essential method for realizing the entire path to enlightenment.

In this prayer we identify the guru with the three objects of refuge, recognizing that without the guru there would be no buddha, dharma or sangha and, consequently, no true happiness.

4   *The seven limbs*

Manjushri, the buddha of wisdom, once gave advice to Je Tzong Khapa on how to attain realizations. He said three things should be practised together: 1) praying sincerely to the guru, seeing him or her as one with the meditational deity; 2) purifying the mind of negative imprints and accumulating merit, that is positive energy and insights; and 3) meditating upon the subjects one wants to realize. Cultivating these three creates the correct causes and conditions for actualizing in our minds the various stages of the path to enlightenment.

The second – purifying negative imprints and accumulating positive energy and insight – is most successfully achieved by the practice of the Seven Limbs. As the body needs its four limbs to be a whole body, so too does any meditation practice need its seven limbs in order to be complete.

Each limb can be practised extensively; they are encapsulated, however, in the Prayer of the Seven Limbs.

i. *Prostration*: Prostrating is a means of showing appreciation and respect for the buddha, dharma and sangha, and is a powerful way to purify negativities, especially pride, which directly prevents our growth of wisdom. There are three ways of making prostrations: physical, verbal and mental.

Physical prostrations can be performed in various ways. The most common method among Tibetan Buddhists is as follows. Begin in a standing position, touch your joined hands to the crown of your head, forehead, throat and heart, then fall to your hands and knees, touch your forehead to the floor and rise.

To do a full-length prostration – more effective in purifying negative energy – again touch your joined hands to the crown of your head, forehead, throat and heart, fall to your hands and knees, then stretch your entire body on the floor, face down, with your arms straight out in front of you. (It would be best to have someone demonstrate these for you, so you can see the correct way to do them.)

Verbal prostration is the recitation of praise to the refuge objects.

Mental prostration is the respect, faith and confidence in the three objects of refuge that accompany physical and verbal prostration. This mental attitude is the essence of the practice and its depth and sincerity determine the power of prostrations.

ii. *Offering*: We delight in giving gifts to friends and sharing pleasant experiences with them. In a spiritual sense we offer beautiful objects, positive thoughts and actions and the pure experience of bliss to our objects of refuge. Making offerings is a powerful antidote to selfishness and attachment and a principal means of accumulating the positive energy crucial to our development of wisdom.

Actual offerings, mentioned in the prayer, are those physically offered (on an altar, for example) to the objects of refuge, while *mentally-transformed offerings* are those we visualize. The essence of any action, and what determines its worth, is the state of one's mind at the time it is done. Simple, insignificant objects can be visualized and offered as the most beautiful sights, sounds, tastes, smells and tangible things imaginable; the benefit of such an offering is enormous.

It is said that a young boy who reverently offered a bowl of dust to the Buddha, visualizing it as gold, was later reborn as the great Indian King Ashoka, largely as a result of the merit of this offering.

Mentally-transformed offerings can be made at any time: whatever beautiful and pleasing object we encounter can be offered in our heart to the objects of refuge, and the merit of the offering dedicated to our attainment of enlightenment for the benefit of all beings. In this way we can be accumulating the causes of enlightenment continually while going about our daily life.

iii. *Confession:* Actions of body, speech and mind that are motivated by delusion – attachment, aversion, confusion, jealousy, pride and the like – are negative, or unskilful, actions because they result in future misfortune and cause us to remain in cyclic existence. However, they can be rectified, and their resultant imprints on the mind purified, through the practice of confession.

There are four steps in this largely internal practice – the four remedial powers – and the success of our purification is measured by the strength and sincerity of our practice of these four.

The power of regret. This is the attitude of first acknowledging and then regretting our negative or unskilful actions, because we see that they are going to cause suffering to ourselves and others in the future. Regret is not like guilt, which involves negative fear and anxiety; rather, it is an intelligent and honest recognition of the nature of our actions and their results.

The power of reliance. When we fall on the ground it hurts us, but we also need to rely on the ground to get back up. Similarly, since we create most negative actions with the three jewels or other sentient beings as object, we rely on these objects to avert the suffering in which such actions result. Hence the power of reliance is taking refuge in buddha, dharma and sangha and regenerating our bodhicitta.

The power of the opponent force. The third step in the process of purification is the practice of positive actions such as offering, prostration, mantra recitation and meditation, especially on emptiness, which counteract the force of previous negative actions.

The power of promise. The final step is the firm determination to avoid doing the same negative actions again. Of course, some actions are easier to avoid than others; it might be realistic to promise never to kill again, but it would be unrealistic to promise never to lose our temper again, for example. In cases like this it would be practical to promise not to do the action for an hour or a day, then gradually extend the period of time as we learn to gain more control over our mind.

Determination is crucial to our success in any venture, especially in our efforts to subdue the mind.

iv. *Rejoicing*: Rejoicing in the well-being of others is a powerful antidote to jealousy and resentment – frequent responses when someone else succeeds or is happy. Jealousy is a tense, unhappy state of mind that cannot bear the happiness of others; rejoicing is light and open, a loving response that allows us to share in their happiness. The benefit, then, is immediate, and we also create the cause to experience happiness ourselves in the future.

We can rejoice at any time, in any place – we don't need to be sitting in meditation. It is one of the easiest, and most necessary, methods of transforming our mind.

v. *Requesting the buddhas not to pass away*: Although the buddhas are always existing and work continuously to help sentient beings, we can connect with them only if we create the appropriate causes. Requesting them to remain in the world and guide us is primarily for our own benefit: it purifies our mind of negative actions done in the past in relation to gurus and buddhas and helps us to open our mind and truly appreciate their help and inspiration. Requesting the buddhas to stay also creates the cause for our own long life.

vi. *Requesting the buddhas to turn the wheel of dharma*: Requesting the buddhas to teach the way to enlightenment enhances our appreciation of the dharma and counteracts past attitudes of disrespect towards spiritual teachings. Especially, it lays the foundation for never being separated from teachers who can guide us spiritually and for always having the teachings available.

vii. *Dedication*: It is very important at the beginning of any meditation or other positive action to have a clear understanding of our motivation; it is equally important to conclude the action by dedicating the merit – the good energy and insight – we have created by doing it. We do this by recalling our initial motivating thought, renewing our aspiration to reach a certain goal, and sending our merit in that direction. Motivation and dedication ensure that our positive energy is not lost and that the results will come. Otherwise, there is no firm imprint put onto the mind, and any good done can easily be destroyed by anger or other negative actions.

The best dedication is to pray that the meditation or action we have just done becomes a cause for our enlightenment for the sake of all sentient beings.

5 *Mandala offering*

The mandala offering involves mentally transforming the entire universe – everything that exists – into a pure realm and offering it to the objects of refuge. The main purpose of doing this practice is to accumulate merit, which is needed in the cultivation of insight and wisdom.

Seeds for our growth on the path to enlightenment are planted in our mind through hearing or reading the teachings. These seeds need the nourishment of merit – strong, positive energy – in order to grow and produce insights and realizations. Offering the mandala is said to be one of the best means of providing this nourishment. It also has immediate benefits: giving from the heart in this way is a remedy for attachment and miserliness.

The prayer is written in terms of Buddhist *abhidharma* cosmology, in which Mount Meru is a jewelled mountain in the centre of the universe and the four continents are different realms of human life. The mandala you offer can accord with either Eastern or Western cosmology, whichever you feel most comfortable with, but the point is to offer *everything* – all the various worlds and realms of living beings and all the beautiful things we enjoy.

Visualize a miniature version of the entire universe in the space in front of you and then transform it into a pure realm. The environment and beings of a pure realm are completely, perfectly beautiful and make the mind peaceful and happy; use your imagination to create a blissful paradise.

Impure objects give rise to attachment, irritation and confusion, while pure objects give rise to clear, positive states of mind, especially the wisdom understanding reality and the experience of great bliss.

Offer this pure land to the refuge objects, without clinging to any part of it, and feel that your gift is accepted with love and the highest appreciation.

The *inner mandala* adds another dimension. Here you bring to mind the people and things – including your body and belongings – for which you have attachment, aversion and indifference. Visualize these objects, transformed into pure objects in the mandala, and offer them all to the buddhas. Having completely given them up, there is now no need to have attachment, dislike or ignorance – the three poisons – towards any person or thing.

6 *Dedication of merit* and
7 *The bodhicitta prayer*

See the explanation of *dedication* under *The seven limbs* on page 153.

At the conclusion of a session of meditation or instruction, the merit generated during the session should be directed to a worthwhile goal – in this case, enlightenment. Reciting these two verses reminds us of the bodhicitta motivation: the aspiration to develop love and compassion for all beings and to attain enlightenment in order to help them. Our merit is thus dedicated to the welfare of others; this is the best dedication we could make.

3 A Short Meditation on the Graduated Path to Enlightenment

This prayer, composed by the fourteenth century Tibetan yogi and scholar, Je Tzong Khapa, summarizes the stages of the graduated path to enlightenment as taught by Shakya-muni Buddha and elucidated by Atisha, the eleventh century Indian pandit.

> The foundation of all knowledge is the kind
>   and venerable guru.
> Please grant me blessings to see clearly
> That trust in him is the root of the path
> And to follow him correctly with great devotion
>   and unfaltering effort.
>
> Please grant me blessings
> To realize that this precious body with freedom
>   is found only once,
> To understand its great meaning and rarity,
> And both day and night
> To cultivate unceasingly the mind that takes
>   hold of its essence.

Please grant me blessings
To realize that the body and life are like
    a water bubble,
To remember how quickly they decay and death
    comes,
And to gain firm unchangeable understanding that
    after death
I must follow black and white karma as the
    shadow follows the body, and thus
To avoid the slightest negative karma
And complete the accumulation of merit.
Bless me always to be cautious and mindful of
    this.

Please grant me blessings
To understand that there is no satisfaction in
    enjoying samsaric pleasures
And that their shortcoming is that they cannot
    be trusted;
May I strive intently for the bliss of
    liberation.
Please bless me to cultivate this wish.

From this pure thought remembrance, awareness
    and great caution arise.
The root of the teachings is keeping the vows
    of individual liberation;
Please grant me blessings to follow this
    essential practice.

Please grant me blessings
To see that all mother beings have fallen into
    the ocean of samsara, just as I have,
To carry the burden of releasing all transmigrators
And to train my mind in supreme bodhicitta.

Please grant me blessings
To see clearly that with bodhicitta alone I
    cannot achieve enlightenment
Without training in the three practices of
    morality
Through the ordinations of the bodhisattvas.
Therefore bless me to observe them with
    intensive effort.

Please grant me blessings
To pacify distractions brought on by wrong
    objects
And, by analyzing the meaning of reality,
To perfect quickly the co-operative paths of
    tranquillity and higher seeing.

Having become a pure vessel through the
    general path,
Please grant me blessings
To enter the holy gateway of the fortunate
    ones
And follow instantly the supreme inseparable
    path.

Please grant me blessings
To gain firm understanding that the basis
    of the two attainments
Is the immaculate word of honour that I have
    pledged
And to protect these pledges at the cost of
    my life.

Please grant me blessings
To recognize the importance of the two stages:
The heart of the tantric path.
Bless me to practise without indolence the
    four sessions of meditation
And to realize the teachings of the holy beings.

May the virtuous guides who lead me on the
    sacred path
And my spiritual friends who practise it
    have long lives.
Please grant me blessings
To pacify completely all outer and inner
    hindrances.

In all my rebirths may I always be united
    with perfect gurus
And enjoy the magnificent dharma;
May I perfectly complete the stages and paths
And may I quickly achieve Vajradhara's state.

4 The Eight Verses and Avalokiteshvara

A good mind, a good heart and warm feelings are most important. If you do not have such a good heart, you yourself cannot function, you cannot be happy and consequently your family, children and neighbours will not be happy either. Thus from nation to nation and continent to continent, everyone's mind will become disturbed and people will not be happy.

But if you do have a good attitude, a good mind, a good heart, the opposite is true. So, in human society, love, compassion and kindness are the most important things; they are truly precious.

It is worthwhile making an effort to develop a good, good heart.

His Holiness the Fourteenth Dalai Lama

Having a good heart means having love – wanting others to be happy – and compassion – wanting them to be free of suffering. To think in this way is the method for achieving our own happiness and the happiness of others. We might know this, but why is it so difficult?

The chief obstacle is our habit of thinking of ourselves first – our self-cherishing attitude. Most of the time we are pre-occupied with keeping ourselves happy and comfortable, trying to fulfil our desires and worrying about our problems, only occasionally finding the energy and the space to really open our hearts to the needs of another.

It is self-cherishing that motivates us to take the biggest piece of cake or the most comfortable chair in the room; to push to the head of the queue or drive as if ours were the only car on the road; to do what we feel like doing without considering how it might affect others. Self-cherishing operates more subtly, too; it lies behind our irritation, pride, jealousy, anxiety and depression. In fact, just about every time we are unhappy or uneasy it is because we are overly concerned with *me*. We feel that unless we take care of ourselves we will not be happy. In fact, the very opposite is true. Ego's appetite is insatiable – trying to fulfil its wishes is a never-ending job. No matter how much we have, ego continuously grows restless and looks for more. We never reach a point where we feel ultimately satisfied, when we can say, "Now I've had enough."

If, on the other hand, we can turn our mind around to think of others and put their needs and desires first, we *will* find peace. There is a serenity that comes from truly cherishing others. By acting always according to what is least disturbing for others, ego is gradually subdued and our life and relationships take on a new dimension.

But the attitude of cherishing others is not based on disliking oneself or suppressing one's feelings. It is developed by gradually coming to recognize that everyone needs love and wants happiness, just as we do; that every being in the universe is part of one big family, that we all depend on each other, that there is no such thing as an outsider; that self-cherishing brings problems and cherishing others brings peace of mind.

It is not easy to develop universal love and compassion, but as soon as we start trying to do so we will see the changes in our life. We need to persevere, and to be kind to ourselves. At times it may seem that we are not getting any better, but this is only because, with deeper conscientiousness, we are now more aware of our mind, of what has been there all the time. We must remember that it takes time and effort to overcome habits built up over a lifetime – over many lifetimes, in fact!

The Tibetan Buddhist tradition contains many practices for improving our attitudes towards others. This meditation belongs to a group of teachings and practices known as thought-transformation, which are concerned with transforming the attitude of self-cherishing into one of cherishing others. The final aim is the development of bodhicitta, the mind aspiring to reach enlightenment for the sake of all beings.

This practice, composed by Lama Thubten Zopa Rinpoche, combines a meditation on Avalokiteshvara, the buddha of compassion, with an eight-verse prayer containing the essence of thought-transformation, written by an eleventh century meditation master, Langri Tangpa Dorje Senge.

THE PRACTICE

Seated comfortably with a quiet, relaxed mind, generate a strong and positive motivation for doing this meditation. Reflect upon the points of the graduated path to enlightenment (page 156) or upon the following.

> It is not enough merely to ensure that I avoid suffering in this and future lifetimes. I must become completely free from cyclic existence, the endless round of death and rebirth.
>
> But this too is inadequate. How can I attain the bliss of liberation, leaving behind all other living beings? Every sentient being has been my mother, not just once but many times in my previous lives, and each has cared for me just like my present

mother, (Think of the kindness of your present mother, all that she has done for you from the time you were born. Think that all beings have been as kind as this.)

I have depended upon them for all the happiness I have ever experienced. All the food I eat, the clothes I wear, the books I read, the shelter I have; all the music, movies and other pleasures I enjoy come to me through the kindness of others.

At the moment, these kind sentient beings are experiencing suffering, and, out of ignorance, are creating the causes for future misery.

Recall the lives of people you know – relatives, friends and neighbours. What problems, physical and mental, are they experiencing? Just as you do not want problems and pain, neither do they. Just as you want happiness and peace of mind, so do they. But do they have any solutions? Do they have any methods to achieve the happiness they want and avoid the suffering they do not want?

Generate the determination to take the responsibility to free *all* sentient beings from their suffering and to lead them to the bliss of enlightenment. But to accomplish this you yourself must be enlightened.

Enlightenment is not without causes and conditions. The principal cause is the loving and compassionate mind of bodhicitta.

Therefore I shall practise the profound teaching on training the mind in bodhicitta.

Visualization: Visualize at the level of your forehead, a body's length away, Avalokiteshvara, the buddha of compassion. (If you have a spiritual teacher, think that Avalokiteshvara is the manifestation of and inseparable from him or her.)

His body is of pure white light and radiates rainbow light of five colours: white, red, blue, green and yellow. He has a gentle smile and looks at you and all other beings with eyes of the greatest compassion.

He has four arms. The hands of the first two are together at his heart and hold a precious jewel that is capable of fulfilling the wishes of every living being. His other right hand holds a crystal rosary and his other left a white lotus. He is seated in the vajra posture on a lotus and a moon–disc and is surrounded by the full moon as his aura.

He wears exquisite silk clothes and precious jewelled ornaments. An antelope skin covers his left shoulder and breast. The entire visualization is of radiant light.

(See page 148 for explanation of the prayers.)

Seven-limb prayer

> I prostrate to you, Avalokiteshvara,
> And present clouds of every type of offering,
>   actual and mentally-transformed.
> I declare all my negative actions accumulated
>   since beginningless time
> And rejoice in the merit of all holy and ordinary
>   beings.
> Please remain until samsara ends
> And turn the wheel of dharma for sentient beings.
> I dedicate the merits created by myself and
>   others to the great enlightenment.

Mandala offering

> The fundamental ground is scented with incense
>   and strewn with flowers,
> Adorned with Mount Meru, the four continents,
>   the sun and the moon.
> I imagine this as a buddha-field and offer it.
> May all living beings enjoy this pure land.

Prayer of request

> May the guru's life be long.

> May all beings throughout infinite space receive
>   happiness and comfort.
> May I and all others, without exception,
>   accumulate merit,
> Purify all obscurations and quickly attain
>   enlightenment.
> Precious guru, please grant blessings for my mind
>   to become dharma,
> For my dharma to become the path,
> For there to be no hindrances to the path, and
> For me to eliminate all wrong conceptions
> And receive immediately the two precious
>   bodhicittas.

Avalokiteshvara is extremely pleased with your request and upon his lotus and moon seat descends to the crown of your head.

The eight verses

Recite the verses, concentrating on their meaning. Take as long as you like with each one.

With each verse, visualize a stream of blissful white nectar pouring out from the syllable *hri* at Avalokiteshvara's heart, flowing into your body through the crown of your head. It fills you completely, purifying all your negativities and obscurations and bringing all realizations – in particular the obscurations and realizations mentioned in the verse you are meditating upon.

> 1 With the thought of attaining enlightenment
>   For the welfare of all beings,
>   Who are more precious than wish-fulfilling jewels,
>   I will constantly practise holding them dear.

Living beings are precious because without them we would have no opportunity to develop generosity, love, patience and other altruistic qualities, or to overcome our selfishness.

The nectar from Avalokiteshvara purifies the self-cherishing thought that prevents me from holding others more dear and bestows the realization of cherishing others more than myself.

2 Whenever I am with others
   I will practise seeing myself as the lowest of all,
   And from the very depths of my heart
   I will recognize others as supreme.

This is a powerful way to counteract our habitual tendency towards finding fault in others and criticizing them. Instead, we should continually recognize their good qualities and potential, and recall our own faults and shortcomings.

The nectar purifies pride and self-cherishing and brings the realization of bodhicitta, which regards others as dear and supreme.

3 In all actions I will examine my mind and
   The moment a delusion arises,
   Endangering myself and others,
   I will firmly confront and avert it.

This verse stresses the importance of mindfulness. Throughout the day, in everything we do – working, talking, watching television, meditating – we should be aware of what is happening in our mind. Whenever a negative thought like anger, jealousy or pride arises, we should take note of it and deal with it as soon as possible. If we do not practise like this, delusions remain in the mind, grow stronger and pollute our every feeling and perception.

The nectar purifies the obscurations that prevent me from confronting and dealing with unsubdued thoughts and brings the realization of bodhicitta and the wisdom of emptiness, which extinguish such thoughts.

4 Whenever I meet a person of bad nature
   Who is overwhelmed by negative energy and intense
      suffering,

I will hold such a rare one dear,
As if I had found a precious treasure.

It is not very difficult to have positive feelings towards people who are kind and good-natured, but our love is really put to the test when we meet people with much negative energy. Because they give us the chance to see how strong our patience and compassion are – and thus bring us down to earth as far as our spiritual development is concerned – we should regard them as rare and precious.

The nectar purifies the self-cherishing thought that prevents me from regarding harmful beings as precious and dear, and brings the realization of bodhicitta, which holds even harmful beings dear.

5 When others, out of jealousy,
   Mistreat me with abuse, slander and scorn,
   I will practise accepting defeat
   And offering the victory to them.

When someone criticizes us, to our face or behind our back, we should not angrily try to defend ourselves or hurl abuse in return. Instead we should remember that any bad experience is the natural outcome of our own past actions –we can probably think of many instances when we criticized others.

We can try to talk with the person who is complaining – not with anger but compassion – to get them to calm down and think more positively, but if they refuse to be reasonable we should just let go and accept the situation. Anyway, it is good to listen with an open mind to criticism – it is often correct and it can always teach us something about ourselves.

The nectar purifies the self-cherishing thought that prevents me from accepting defeat and giving the victory to others, and brings the realizations that enable me to do this.

6 When someone I have benefited
   And in whom I have placed great trust

Hurts me very badly,
I will practise seeing that person as my supreme
  teacher.

Every good or bad experience that occurs in our life is the
result of our past actions, so there is really no such thing as
undeserved harm. This idea may be difficult to accept, especially when the harm comes from someone whom we have
helped and from whom we expect at least gratitude. But it is
a question of becoming familiar with the law of cause and
effect – we must necessarily have created the cause to be
harmed. Also, if we have good understanding of the importance of developing patience, we will be able to see that
someone who harms us is giving us a valuable teaching on
the spiritual path.

The nectar purifies the self-cherishing thought that prevents me from regarding harmful beings as my spiritual
teachers, and brings the attainment of the bodhisattva's perfection of patience, which enables me to do this.

7 In short, I will offer directly and indirectly
  Every benefit and happiness to all beings, my
    mothers.
  I will practise in secret taking upon myself
  All their harmful actions and suffering.

The essence of thought transformation is exchanging self
for others – replacing the attitude of cherishing oneself with
that of cherishing others. Normally we work on making
ourselves happy and avoiding problems, even if it means
hurting others, but here we reverse our priorities; we aspire
to give happiness to others and to take on their problems,
indifferent to our own welfare. This meditation is an internal
one, involving a change in our state of mind; it is therefore
"secret," not something that everyone can see us practising.

The nectar purifies the self-cherishing thought that prevents me from taking upon myself all beings' harmful actions

and sufferings, and brings the realization of bodhicitta, which offers happiness to them and takes on their suffering.

8 Through perceiving all phenomena as illusory I
    will keep these practices
  Undefiled by the stains of the eight worldly concerns,
    And, free from clinging, I will release all beings
  From the bondage of the disturbing unsubdued mind
    and karma.

When our motivation for doing something involves any of the eight worldly concerns – attachment to pleasure, praise, gain and fame, and aversion to pain, blame, loss and notoriety – the action is non-dharma, non-spiritual. By realizing the illusory, dream-like nature of all things and all situations, we naturally learn to let go and cling less tightly to such concerns.

The final aim of this practice is to free ourselves from ignorance, self-cherishing and all negative energy in order to help others become free, too.

The nectar purifies the self-cherishing thought and self-grasping ignorance that prevent me from seeing all things as illusory, and brings the realization of emptiness, which frees me from the bondage of the unsubdued mind and karma.

Completion: Make the following request from the depths of your heart.

  To you, greatly compassionate one, I request:
  Please extend your holy hand and lead me and all
    beings
  To the blissful pure realm after this life.
  Please be our spiritual friend in all lives
  And lead us quickly to enlightenment.

Avalokiteshvara accepts your request. A stream of nectar flows from his heart into you, completely filling your body and mind. All obscurations, negative imprints and diseases are purified instantly. Your body becomes crystal-clear. Then Avalokiteshvara melts into light and absorbs into you.

Now you are Avalokiteshvara, your body, speech and mind indistinguishably one with his holy body, speech and mind. You are surrounded in all directions by all sentient beings.

Avalokiteshvara's mantra: Now, while reciting the mantra *om mani padme hum,* visualize countless rays of light radiating from your heart, each with a tiny Avalokiteshvara at its tip. These compassionate buddhas settle above the heads of all sentient beings and with streams of nectar purify their negativities and obscurations. Finally, they absorb into the sentient beings, who all become Avalokiteshvara.

Dedication prayers

> May the suffering and causes of suffering of all
>   beings
> Ripen on me now.
> May all beings receive the results, my happiness,
> And its cause, my merits.

> May the supreme jewel bodhicitta
> That has not arisen, arise and grow;
> And may that which has arisen not diminish
> But increase more and more.

> Without being discouraged, even for a moment,
> May I completely renounce selfish actions
> And practise, for the sake of others, the bodhi-
>   sattva's great deeds,
> Which are like the holy actions of the kind
>   founder, Shakyamuni Buddha.

> Through these merits
> May I quickly attain the state of the Great
> Compassionate One,
> And lead all living beings, the supreme noble ones,
> Into that enlightened state.

5   *Prayer to Tara*

Why is it that some people succeed in nearly everything they set out to do while others fail constantly? We say that those who succeed are "lucky," but Buddhism explains that in the past they have created the causes to experience their success – otherwise they would not be experiencing it now.

If we want to meet with fortunate, satisfying experiences we must create the necessary causes. This is true for any activity – a business venture, sport, or spiritual practice. We tend to find that the more difficult the goal, the greater the obstacles. An effective method for overcoming these problems and achieving success is making prayers and requests to Tara, the Liberator.

Tara is a manifestation of the wisdom, compassion, love and, in particular, the skilful activity of all enlightened beings. Each detail of her image represents a different aspect of the path: for example, her green colour symbolizes her ability to act. Her right hand is in the gesture of granting sublime realizations and her left in the gesture of refuge. Her female form demonstrates that enlightenment is attainable by all – women and men alike.

The practice given here involves repetition of a five-line

prayer, which is the essence of the prayer known as the *Twenty-one Verses in Praise of Tara,* and contains her mantra, *om tare tuttare ture soha* (pronounced *om ta-ray too-ta-ray too-ray so-ha*).

There is a story about how this five-line prayer originated. In the tenth century, the translator for Atisha, the great Indian teacher who lived in Tibet, became ill. Dromtönpa, Atisha's disciple, predicted that if the translator recited the *Twenty-one Verses in Praise of Tara* ten thousand times, he would recover from his illness. The man was too sick to recite this long prayer, so Atisha, who had direct communication with Tara, requested her advice. She gave him the five-line prayer, a single repetition of which is equivalent to recitation of the twenty-one verses. The translator completed the ten thousand repetitions and soon after recovered fully from his illness.

This practice has been compiled by Lama Thubten Zopa Rinpoche as a way for us to open our hearts to Tara's incredibly kind, inspiring energy.

THE PRACTICE

Visualize Tara in the space before you, emerald green in colour, seated on a lotus and moon (see page 118). She is a manifestation of all the buddhas' ominiscience, love and compassion, and is of the nature of light, not solid or concrete. Her left leg is drawn up, signifying her complete control over desire, and her right leg extended, indicating that she is ready to rise to the aid of all beings. Her left hand is at her heart in the refuge gesture: palm facing outward, thumb and ring finger joined, and the remaining three fingers raised. Her right hand is on her right knee in the gesture of granting sublime realizations: palm facing outward, thumb and first finger touching, and the remaining fingers pointing down. In each hand she holds the stem of a blue utpala flower, symbol of the unblocking of the central channel. She is beautifully adorned with silk garments and jewel ornaments, and her smiling face radiates love and compassion.

All sentient beings, in human form, surround you: the people you are close to are behind you, those you do not like are in front of you, and all the rest are on either side of you. You are completely surrounded by all sentient beings, as far as the eye can see.

Everyone joins you in reciting the following prayers.

Refuge and bodhicitta

> I take refuge until I am enlightened
> In the buddhas, the dharma and the sangha.
> Through the merit I create by practising giving
>   and the other perfections,
> May I attain buddhahood for the sake of all
>   sentient beings.

The four immeasurable thoughts

> May all sentient beings have happiness and the
>   causes of happiness;
> May all sentient beings be free from suffering and
>   the causes of suffering;
> May all sentient beings never be separated from
>   the happiness that knows no suffering;
> May all sentient beings abide in equanimity, free
> from attachment and anger, which hold some
>   close and others distant.

The seven limbs

> Reverently I prostrate with my body, speech and
>   mind
> And present clouds of every type of offering,
>   actual and mentally-transformed.
> I declare all my negative actions accumulated since
>   beginningless time
> And rejoice in the merit of all holy and ordinary
>   beings.

Please remain until samsara ends
And turn the wheel of dharma for sentient beings.
I dedicate the merits created by myself and others
    to the great enlightenment.

Mandala offering

The fundamental ground is scented with incense
    and strewn with flowers,
Adorned with Mount Meru, the four continents,
    the sun and the moon.
I imagine this as a buddha-land and offer it.
May all living beings enjoy this pure realm.

Prayer to Tara

Now recall any special request you want to make – success in your spiritual or worldly activities, the health and long life of your relatives, friends or yourself, or anything at all that you want. With these needs in mind, recite the short prayer to Tara as many times as you can, either while remaining seated or making prostrations.

Om, I and all prostrate to the liberator, the
    fully-realized, transcendent subduer.
I prostrate to the glorious mother who liberates
    with *tare*;
You are the mother who eliminates all fears with
    tuttare;
You are the mother who grants all success with
    ture;
To *soha* and the other syllables we offer the
    greatest homage.

As you recite the prayer visualize rays of light with nectar running down them (like raindrops running down a wire) emanating from the point where Tara's left thumb and ring finger touch. The rays and nectar flow continuously, reaching you and all the beings surrounding you, purifying your hindrances to dharma practice and the obscurations to liberation and enlightenment.

Remember the problems of all the people you are praying for. Think also of the sufferings and troubles being experienced by the sentient beings surrounding you: people fighting wars, feeling ill or lonely; those full of anger, pride or jealousy. As the rays and nectar enter their bodies and minds, their suffering and the causes of their suffering are completely extinguished. All sentient beings become totally liberated.

Think with deep conviction that Tara has accepted your requests and answered your prayers. During the first half of your recitation you can visualize the purification described above, and during the second half you can visualize that you and all beings become one with Tara: with each prayer an identical Tara emanates from the Tara visualized in front of you and dissolves into you and everyone else. You all become completely one with Tara's holy body, speech and mind.

Dedication of merit

> Through these merits
> May I quickly attain the state of Tara
> And lead all living beings, without exception,
> Into that enlightened state.
>
> May the supreme jewel bodhicitta
> That has not arisen, arise and grow;
> And may that which has arisen not diminish
> But increase more and more.

Explanation of the prayer

Om contains three sounds: *ah, oh* and *mm,* and signifies the immeasureable qualities of the enlightened beings' holy bodies, speech and minds. According to the tantric teachings of Buddha, the paths included in the mantra *om tare tuttare ture soha* lead to the omniscient state of mind. By actualizing these paths in our mind we purify our body, speech and mind and transform them into Tara's holy body, speech and mind.

Here, *om* is the goal and *tare tuttare ture* is the path.

Tare: "She who liberates." Usually, "Tara" means to liberate from unfortunate rebirths, the sufferings of cyclic existence, and the subtle trap of nirvana.

Although one might become free from cyclic existence and attain nirvana, it takes a long time to rouse oneself from this blissful state of peace and begin to work for sentient beings. Compared with the motivation of attaining enlightenment in order to work for others, the goal of attaining nirvana for oneself alone is limited. Thus Tara frees us not only from cyclic existence but also from the blissful state of peace and leads us to enlightenment.

This is the usual meaning of the first *tare* in the mantra. It represents everything from which we should be liberated, the path that liberates, and the goal to which Tara leads us: the ominscient state of enlightenment.

Here, however, the meaning of *tare* is explained as being liberation from cyclic existence, the first of the four truths – suffering (see page 74).

Tuttare: "Who eliminates all fears." Tara is said to free us from eight "fears," or the sufferings of eight kinds of delusion, each of which is compared to an external cause of fear: the suffering of attachment, which is like a great flood; the suffering of anger, which is like fire; the suffering of ignorance, which is like an elephant; the suffering of jealousy, which is like a snake; the suffering of pride, which is like a lion; the suffering of miserliness, which is like imprisoning chains; the suffering of wrong views, which is like a thief; and the suffering of doubt, which is like a ghost. If we take refuge in Tara, recite her mantra and practise her method, she will release us from not only the internal sufferings of the delusions but also from external dangers such as floods, fires and thieves.

Thus, with *tuttare* Tara liberates us from the true causes of suffering (the second of the four noble truths) – karma and the delusions that give rise to karma. By reciting it our fears can be dispelled, which indicates that Tara leads us to the true path, the absolute dharma – the actual remedy for the causes of suffering.

Ture: "Who grants all success." Here, success refers to the goals of practitioners having the three levels of motivation; a fortunate birth, the goal of the initial level of motivation; nirvana, the goal of the intermediate level of motivation; and enlightenment, the goal of the highest level of motivation. "All success" also refers to success in all pursuits of this life – in relationships, in business, in finding perfect conditions for our dharma practice and in accomplishing our dharma goals.

Soha: Each word of the mantra – from *om* to *soha* – performs a particular function, as explained above; each brings great benefit. Thus "to *soha* and the other syllables we offer the greatest homage."

Soha itself means "May the blessings of Tara that are contained in the mantra *om tare tuttare ture* take root in our hearts." If we want to grow apples in our garden, we should plant the root of an apple tree. Similarly, if we want to attain enlightenment we should plant in our heart the root of the complete path, which is contained in the mantra *om tare tuttare ture soha*. By praying to Tara and reciting her mantra we receive her blessings; through Tara's blessings entering our heart we are able to generate the entire path to enlightenment. By generating the path – method and wisdom – in our minds, our impure body, speech and mind are purified and transformed into Tara's holy body, speech and mind.

6 *Vajrasattva Purification*

Why, when we sit down to meditate, does our mind wander helplessly here and there? Why is it so difficult to control the mind and attain realizations? Perhaps we imagine that things were easier before we started to meditate!

Transforming the mind is not easy, so it is not surprising that we experience obstacles and problems. It is not that we lack wisdom or the ability to meditate properly, to penetrate deep into the mind; rather, it is because of the negative energy of our delusions, our distorted conceptions and emotions, which have been accumulating since beginningless time.

When we sit down to meditate, this energy manifests physically as discomfort or restlessness and mentally as sleepiness, agitation, tension or doubt. Our weak wisdom-flame exists but is no match for this dark storm of negative energy.

It is possible to still the storm, to purify the negative energy that prevents us from actualizing the path to enlightenment. An especially powerful Vajrayana method is the practice associated with the buddha Vajrasattva (Tibetan: Dorje Sempa). It is said to be as effective in burning away delusions and negative energy as is a great fire in burning away thousands of acres of forest.

One of the characteristics of the result of any action is that it increases with time, in the same way that one fruit seed results in many fruits. It is obvious, then, that to prevent the results of negative actions increasing it is necessary to purify our minds of imprints left by negative actions of body, speech and mind.

Recitation of the Vajrasattva mantra at least twenty-one times at the end of each day is said to prevent the power of that day's negative energy increasing. Recitation of the mantra one hundred-thousand times, in the right conditions and with the right state of mind, has the power to purify all negative imprints completely.

Complete purification of our negative energy – which ensures that we will never need to experience the results of our negative actions – depends on strong, pure confession. The four steps in this largely internal practice are known as the four remedial powers (see page 152). The two meditations here – by Lama Thubten Zopa Rinpoche – combine visualization of Vajrasattva with the four powers; one is done while sitting and the other while prostrating.

THE PRACTICE WHILE SITTING
The power of reliance

Visualize about four inches above the crown of your head an open white lotus bearing a moon disc, upon which is seated Vajrasattva. He is white, translucent and adorned with beautiful ornaments and clothes of celestial silk. Every aspect of this visualization is the nature of light. He has two hands, crossed at his heart: the right holds a vajra, symbolic of great bliss; the left holds a bell, symbolic of the wisdom of emptiness. The vajra and bell together signify his attainment of the enlightened state, the inseparable unity of the wisdom and form bodies. At his heart is a moon-disc with the seed syllable *hum* at its centre and the letters of the hundred-syllable mantra of Vajrasattva standing clockwise around its edge.

Holding this visualization clearly in your mind, recite the following prayer for the taking of refuge and the generation of bodhicitta.

> I take refuge in the sublime precious three;
> I will liberate all sentient beings
> And lead them to enlightenment;
> Thus perfectly do I generate bodhicitta.

The power of regret

Recollect with deep regret the specific negativities you have created. Then meditate deeply on the meaning of the following:

> The negative karma I have accumulated through-out beginningless time is as extensive as the trea-sury of a great king. Although each negative action leads to countless aeons of suffering, it seems that I am constantly striving to create noth-ing but negative actions. Even though I am trying to avoid non-virtue and practise positive acts, day and night without respite negativities and moral downfalls come to me like rainfall. I lack the abil-ity to purify these faults so that no trace of them remains; with these negative imprints still in my mind, I could suddenly die and find myself falling to an unfortunate rebirth. What can I do? Please Vajrasattva, with your great compassion, guide me from such misery!

The power of the opponent force

Visualize light radiating in all directions, from the *hum* at Vajrasattva's heart requesting the buddhas to bestow their blessings. They accept the request and send white rays of light and nectar, the essence of which is the knowledge of their body, speech and mind. This light and nectar fall like a rain of milk and are absorbed into the *hum* and mantra at Vajrasattva's heart. Filling his holy body completely, they

enhance the magnificence of his appearance, and increase the brilliance of the mantra until it shines with the light of one hundred-thousand moons reflecting off snowy mountains.

Then, while reciting the hundred-syllable mantra, visualize that white rays of light and nectar stream down continuously from the *hum* and mantra at Vajrasattva's heart. They penetrate the crown of your head, filling your body and mind with infinite bliss.

> *Om vajrasattva samaya manu palaya / vajrasattva deno pathita dido may bhawa / suto kayo may bhawa / supo kayo may bhawa / anu rakto may bhawa / sarwa siddhi may par ya tse / sarwa karma su tsa may / tsi tam shri yam kuru hum / ha ha ha ha ho / bhagawan / sarwa tathagata / vajra ma may mu tsa / vajra bhawa maha samaya sattva / ah hum pay /*

Continue reciting the mantra and visualize the flow of light and nectar, while also performing the following four visualizations in turn.

Purification of body. Your delusions and negativities in general, and particularly those of the body, take the form of black ink, and sicknesses and afflictions caused by spirits take the form of scorpions, snakes, frogs and crabs. Flushed out by the light and nectar, they all leave your body through the lower openings, like filthy water flowing from a drain-pipe. You are now completely emptied of these problems; they no longer exist anywhere.

Purification of speech. Your delusions and the imprints of negativities of speech take the form of liquid tar. The light and nectar fill your body as water fills a dirty glass: the negativities, like the dirt in the glass, rise to the top and flow out through the upper openings of your body. You are completely emptied of these problems; they no longer exist anywhere.

Purification of the mind. Your delusions and imprints of mental negativities appear as darkness at your heart. When struck by the forceful stream of light and nectar, the darkness instantly disappears. You are completely emptied of these problems; they no longer exist anywhere.

Simultaneous purification. Finally, visualize these three purifications simultaneously; they sweep away the subtle obscurations that prevent you from seeing correctly all that exists. You are completely emptied of these problems; they no longer exist anywhere.

If you are short of time, or just lazy, and unable to do the preceding visualizations, there is a simplified, alternative visualization:

All the delusions and negativities that you have collected over beginningless lifetimes appear as darkness at your heart. As you recite the mantra, immeasurable, powerful rays of white light and nectar pour down from Vajrasattva's heart and penetrate the crown of your head. Instantly, the darkness at your heart is dispelled, just as the darkness in a room vanishes the moment a light is switched on.

The power of promise

Make the following promise to Vajrasattva, specifying the period for which you intend to keep it:

"I shall not create these negative actions from now until...."

Vajrasattva is extremely pleased and says: "Child of the essence, all your negativities, obscurations and degenerated vows have now been completely purified."

Then Vajrasattva melts into light and dissolves into you. Your body, speech and mind become inseparably one with Vajrasattva's holy body, speech and mind.

At the conclusion of the meditation, recite the following prayers:

> Through this virtuous action
> May I quickly become Vajrasattva
> And lead every living being, without exception,
> To his enlightened state.

> May the supreme jewel bodhicitta
> That has not arisen, arise and grow;
> And may that which has arisen not diminish
> But increase more and more.

THE PRACTICE WHILE PROSTRATING
The power of reliance

Visualize Vajrasattva in front of you, and all sentient beings in human form surrounding you. Take refuge and think:

> In order to transform my body, speech and mind into the holy body, speech and mind of Vajrasattva for the sole purpose of enlightening all mother sentient beings, with great respect I will now make prostrations.

The power of regret

Recollect with deep regret the negativities you have created with body, speech and mind.

The power of the opponent force

While you prostrate, recite the Vajrasattva mantra. Visualize the mantra as a stream of white letters, made of light, flowing from a white *om* at Vajrasattva's brow and absorbing into your own brow, completely purifying the obscurations of your body.

At the same time, visualize the mantra as a stream of red letters, made of light, flowing from a red *ah* at Vajrasattva's throat and dissolving into your own throat, completely purifying the obscurations of your speech.

Simultaneously, visualize the mantra as a stream of blue letters, made of light, flowing from a blue *hum* at Vajrasattva's heart and dissolving into your own heart, completely purifying the obscurations of your mind.

As you purify yourself in this way, visualize all sentient beings around you also prostrating and purifying their own body, speech and mind.

After each prostration, a replica of Vajrasattva absorbs into you and every other being. Think that your body, speech and mind and those of all beings have been completely purified and are one with Vajrasattva's holy body, speech and mind.

The power of promise

At the end of the session, make the promise, visualize Vajrasattva dissolving into you and all sentient beings, and dedicate the merit of the practice with the two dedication prayers.

Explanation of the mantra

Om signifies the qualities of the buddhas' body, speech and mind. It also stands for what is auspicious and of highest value.

Vajrasattva (Tibetan: *Dorje Sempa*) The courageous one who has inseparable transcendent wisdom.

Samaya A pledge that cannot be transgressed.

Manu palaya Lead me along the path you took to enlightenment.

Vajrasattva deno pa To be closer to the vajra holy mind.

Titha Please make me abide.

Dido Firm; stable because of its relations to the absolute nature.

May I

Bhawa Please grant me the ability to realize the nature of phenomena.

Suto kayo may bhawa Please have the nature of being exceedingly pleased with me.

Supo kayo may bhawa May I be in the nature of the highly developed great bliss.

Anu rakto may bhawa Please be in the nature of the love that leads me to your state.

Sarwa siddhi may par ya tsa Please grant me all the actual attainments.

Sarwa karma su tsa may Please grant me all the virtuous actions.

Tsi tam shri yam kuru Please grant me all your glorious qualities.

Hum Seed syllable signifying the vajra holy mind.

Ha ha ha ha ho Signifies the five transcendent wisdoms.

Bhagawan One who has destroyed every obscuration, attained all realizations and passed beyond all suffering.

Sarwa tathagata All those who have gone in the space of emptiness just as it is.

Vajra Inseparable.

Ma may mu tsa Do not abandon me.

Vajra Bhawa The nature of inseparability.

Maha samaya sattva The great courageous one having the pledge, the holy mind.

Ah Seed syllable signifying the vajra holy speech.

Hum Signifies the transcendent wisdom of great bliss.

Pay Clarifies our understanding of the transcendent wisdom of inseparable bliss and emptiness. It also destroys the dualistic mind that is opposite to that wisdom.

In summary, the mantra means: O great courageous one whose holy mind is in the vajra nature of all buddhas, having destroyed every obscuration, attained all realizations and passed beyond all suffering, gone just as it is – do not forsake me but liberate me, please, according to your pledge.

The short Vajrasattva mantra is: *om vajrasattva hum*.

7 *The Eight Mahayana Precepts*

Keeping vows, or precepts, of morality is the most effective way to remove hindrances to spiritual realizations. Hindrances are the imprints left on our mindstream by unskilful actions of body, speech and mind. By consciously avoiding negative actions we naturally cease creating more hindrances and purify those of the past, thus clearing our mind for the attainment of realizations.

There are various levels of vows in the Mahayana tradition of Buddhism, such as the vows of full ordination taken for life by monks and nuns, the vows of novice monks and nuns, and vows taken by lay people. The taking of vows in a formal ceremony before one's teachers or the visualized buddhas is considered to have more power and meaning for the mind than simply avoiding certain actions in an informal way. Furthermore, if the vows are taken with the Mahayana motivation of bodhicitta, that is for the welfare of all living beings, the beneficial results are infinite.

It is important to study the benefits of keeping vows and the disadvantages of breaking them (explained below) so that when you do take vows you have full understanding of what you are doing.

The Eight Mahayana Precepts are a set of vows that anyone can take for a period of twenty-four hours. They can be taken any time, but the days of the new, full and quarter moons are recommended. The ceremony should be performed early in the morning, before dawn (or "while it is still too dark to see the lines on the palm of your outstretched hand"), and the vows should be maintained until sunrise the following day.

The first time you take the precepts you should do so from a person who has received the oral transmission of the practice, regarding that person as Buddha and imagining that you are making your promises to him. Thereafter, you can perform the ceremony yourself, reciting the prayers before an image of your teacher or the Buddha, again imagining that you are taking the vows from Buddha himself.

If you break any of the vows during the day, you should purify the transgression as soon as possible with the four opponent powers (see page 152). Increased familiarity with keeping precepts will lessen the chances of careless, unconscious transgression.

The benefits of keeping precepts: Buddha has said, "Keeping precepts is much more beneficial than making many offerings to all the buddhas over as many aeons as there are grains of sand in the Ganges." And, according to one great Indian pandit, "Keeping the eight precepts for just one day brings greater benefit than making charity for one hundred years."

By keeping precepts we will develop a clear, uncluttered mind and thus find it easier to meditate; avoid unfortunate rebirths and obtain human rebirths with all the necessary conditions for dharma practice; meet perfect teachers in future lives, thereby giving ourselves the opportunity to receive further teachings and attain spiritual realization – Maitreya, the future Buddha, said, "Any follower of Shakyamuni Buddha who keeps the eight precepts will be reborn as one of those around me." And we will attain liberation from cyclic existence and finally the goal of enlightenment, actualizing the knowledge and perfections of the Buddha's holy body, speech and mind.

The disadvantages of breaking precepts: Having promised not to do a particular negative action and later doing it results in greater negative karma than doing it under ordinary circumstances. This should be clearly understood before we commit ourselves to any vows. Taking and then breaking precepts amounts to lying to the buddhas; moreover, because they are taken in order to benefit all sentient beings, breaking precepts is like lying to all sentient beings as well. Such negligence leaves deep negative imprints on the mindstream that will lead to future misfortune.

If precepts are broken, we will not receive the benefits mentioned above. In addition, we will remain longer in cyclic existence and experience the sufferings of unfortunate rebirths. If we are close to attaining realizations, breaking precepts will cause us to lose the insight we have already developed. It is essential, therefore, to take the precepts seriously and with proper understanding.

The eight precepts

1. To avoid killing, that is causing the death of another living being directly or indirectly.

2. To avoid stealing, that is taking something of value that belongs to another without their permission. This includes borrowing with the clear intention not to return the object.

3. To avoid sexual intercourse and any other type of sexual contact, including self-stimulation.

4. To avoid telling lies, that is deceiving another by your actions of body, speech and mind, or having someone lie on your behalf. It includes lying by implication, for example, remaining silent in answer to a question, thus allowing someone to draw a false conclusion.

5. To avoid intoxicants, that is alcohol, tobacco, drugs, and so forth.

6. To avoid eating more than one meal during the twenty-

four-hour period. The meal should be taken before noon and once you have stopped eating for more than thirty minutes the meal is considered finished. Thereafter light fluids such as tea and coffee can be taken, but not undiluted whole milk or fruit juice with pulp. You should also avoid eating certain "black" foods, such as meat, eggs, onions, garlic and radishes.

7. To avoid sitting on a high, expensive bed or seat with proud motivation. Ornate or jewelled seats and animal-skin covers should also be avoided.

8. To avoid wearing jewellery, perfume and similiar adornments, and to avoid singing, dancing or playing music with attachment.

For a precept to be broken, four conditions must be met.

1. The motivation for the action should be a negative attitude such as attachment, aversion and so forth.

2. There should be an object of the action, for example, a being that is killed, an object that is stolen, and so forth.

3. One should carry out the action or tell another to do it.

4. The action should be completed, for example the being you kill should die before you, or you should have the thought "this is mine" regarding a stolen object.

The heaviness or lightness of the action is determined by the intensity of these four factors. For example, an action motivated by intense anger is more serious than the same action performed out of ignorance; or killing a human being is more serious than killing an insect. In order to understand this subject more fully, one should make a study of karma, the law of cause and effect.

THE CEREMONY
Preliminary prayers, said while standing:

Refuge in the guru

> The guru is buddha, the guru is dharma,
> The guru is sangha also;

The guru is the creator of all happiness:
In all gurus I take refuge. (3 times)

Generating bodhicitta

In order to attain success for myself and
    others
I will generate the mind of enlightenment. (3 times)

Purifying the environment

May the land become pure,
Without roughness or thorns;
Even, like the palm of the hand,
And smooth in nature, like lapis lazuli.

Offering prayer

May the offering materials of gods and humans,
Those actually arranged and those mentally
    transformed,
As well as clouds of supreme offerings of the
    bodhisattva Samantabadhra
Pervade the entire expanse of limitless space.

Mantra to bless and increase the offerings

*Om namo bagawatay / benzay sarwa parma dana /
tathagata ya / arhatay / samyak sambuddhaya /
tayata / om bendzay bendzay / maha bendzay /
maha taydza bendzay / maha biya bendzay / maha
bodhitsita bendzay / maha bodhi mendo pasam damana
bendzay / sarwa karma awa / rana bisho dana bendzay
soha /* (3 times)

Expressing the power of truth

By the power of the truth of the three jewels
And the blessings of all buddhas and bodhisattvas;
By the great strength of the accomplishments of
    the merits of method and transcendent wisdom
And the inconceivable pure sphere of dharma,
May these visualized offerings become real.

Invocation

> You, protector of all living beings without
>   exception,
> Who have vanquished the unbearable host of
>   hindrances
> And perfectly understood all that exists;
> Together with your retinue, please descend to
>   this place.

Now do three prostrations whilst repeating the mantra

> *om namo manjushriye namo sushriye namo uttama
> shriye soha*

then sit down.

The seven limbs

> Reverently I prostrate with my body, speech and
>   mind
> And present clouds of every type of offering,
>   actual and mentally-transformed.
> I declare all my negative actions accumulated since
>   beginningless time
> And rejoice in the merit of all holy and ordinary
>   beings.
> Please remain until samsara ends
> And turn the wheel of dharma for sentient beings.
> I dedicate the merit created by myself and others to
>   the great enlightenment.

Mandala offering

> The fundamental ground is scented with incense
>   and strewn with flowers,
> Adorned with Mount Meru, the four continents,
>   the sun and the moon.
> I imagine this as a buddha-land and offer it.
> May all living beings enjoy this pure realm.

The objects of my attachment, aversion and
   ignorance – friends, enemies and strangers –
My body, wealth and enjoyments;
Without any sense of loss I offer this collection.
Please accept it with pleasure
And bless me with freedom from the three
   poisons.

I send forth this jewelled mandala to you precious
   gurus.

Taking the ordination

Repeat the following prayer three times.

All you buddhas and bodhisattvas residing in the
ten directions, please pay attention to me! As the
tathagatas, the foe-destroyers and the completely
perfected buddhas of the past who, like the heav-
enly steed and the great elephant, accomplished
their objective and did their task, laid down their
load, achieved their own purpose, consumed their
ties to samsara; as they possessed perfect speech, a
mind properly liberated, a wisdom properly liberated; as they took correctly the Mahayana precepts
for the sake of all sentient beings, in order to
benefit them, in order to liberate them, in order to
eliminate their famine, in order to eliminate their
disease, in order to effect their perfecting the qualities on the side of enlightenment, and in order to
bring about their ascertainment of the highest perfect enlightenment; in the same way, from this
moment until sunrise tomorrow, I, (say your
name), will also accept correctly the Mahayana
precepts for the sake of all sentient beings, in order
to benefit them, in order to liberate them, in order
to eliminate their famine, in order to eliminate
their disease, in order to effect their perfecting the

qualities on the side of enlightenment, and in order to bring about their ascertainment of the highest perfect enlightenment.

The prayer of commitment to keeping the precepts

From now on I will not kill, or take another's property. I will not engage in sexual activity. I will not speak 'false words. I will completely avoid alcohol, which is taught to have many faults. I will avoid food at an improper time; perfumes, beads and ornaments, singing and dancing, and so forth. By avoiding killing and the like, just as the foe-destroyers never performed killing and the like, may I quickly obtain the highest enlightenment. May I be freed from the ocean of samsara, the world that stirs up many miseries.

Mantra to purify broken precepts

Om ahmoga shila sambara bara bara maha shuda sato payma bibu kita budza dara dara samanta ahwalokite hum pay soha
Repeat it seven or twenty-one times.

Dedication prayers

By having the flawless morality of the dharma law and a morality kept pure, by a morality which is without conceit, may I fulfil the perfection of morality.

May the supreme jewel bodhicitta
That has not arisen, arise and grow;
And may that which has arisen not diminish
But increase more and more.

In all my rebirths may I always be united with
    perfect gurus
And enjoy the magnificent dharma;
May I perfectly complete the stages and paths
And may I quickly achieve Vajradhara's state.

By these virtues may all beings
Perfect the two accumulations of merit and
    wisdom,
And obtain the two holy bodies
Born from merit and wisdom.

Just as the brave Manjushri has realized –
As has Samantabhadra – things as they are,
I dedicate all these merits in the best way,
That I may follow after them.

I dedicate all these roots of virtue
With the dedication praised as the best
By the victorious thus-gone-ones of the
    three times,
And so that I might perform noble works.

At the end of the day, dedicate the merit of keeping the precepts.

Through these merits, may I quickly attain enlightenment by realizing renunciation, bodhicitta and emptiness, for the sake of all sentient beings.

8   The Bodhisattva's Confession of Moral Downfalls

Pure moral discipline is essential for the realization of the graduated stages of the path to enlightenment. Moral discipline, one of the six perfections, or practices of a bodhisattva, entails creating positive actions and purifying negative actions and broken vows. *The Bodhisattva's Confession of Moral Downfalls* (also known as *The Confession Prayer to the Thirty-five Buddhas*) is just one of the many methods used for purification.

Negative actions can be purified fully only if the four remedial powers are used (see page 152). These four powers are included in the confession prayer: the *power of reliance* in the explicit expression of refuge in the gurus, buddhas, dharma and sangha; the *power of the opponent force* in the recitation of the names of the thirty-five buddhas; the *power of regret* in the recollection of the negative actions we created in the past; and the *power of promise* in the line "... from now on I promise to refrain from these actions." To make the four powers complete, we should begin by generating pure bodhicitta motivation for doing the practice.

This method is especially powerful if practised first thing in the morning to purify any negativities created during the night, and last thing at night to purify negativities created during the day. The most effective way to use the prayer is to recite it while mentally visualizing the thirty-five buddhas and physically making prostrations (see page 145). In this way one's mind, speech and body all take part in the purification process.

THE PRACTICE

Visualize the thirty-five buddhas. Shakyamuni Buddha, the central figure, is visualized in the space before you and slightly above your head. He is seated on a throne made of pearl, which is supported by an elephant. Pearl, being white, symbolizes the complete purification of negativities, and the elephant, being a powerful animal, symbolizes powerful purification. Buddha sits in the vajra posture, wearing the robes of a monk; his right hand is in the earth-touching gesture while his left is in his lap, holding a bowl filled with nectar. Thirty-four rays of light emanate from his heart: ten upwards, ten downwards and seven to either side. At the end of each ray is a pearl throne supported by an elephant. The thirty-four remaining buddhas are seated on these thrones in the vajra posture; all are in the aspect of monks.

As you recite the prayer, rays of light flow from the buddhas, purifying all negativities of your body, speech and mind. Immediately, your negative imprints disappear completely, just as the darkness in a room vanishes the moment a light is switched on. Feel that your body and mind become completely empty and pure in nature.

First, make three prostrations, each time reciting the following mantra:

Om namo manjushriye namo sushriye namo uttama shriye soha

Continue to prostrate while reciting the prayer below in English, or Tibetan (see page 210). If you have not memorized the prayer, read it through once, make prostrations reciting only the names of the buddhas, and when you have finished prostrating read the whole prayer once more.

I, (say your name), throughout all times, take refuge in the gurus; I take refuge in the buddhas; I take refuge in the dharma; I take refuge in the sangha.

To the Founder, the Transcendent Destroyer, the One Gone Beyond, the Foe Destroyer, the Fully Enlightened One, the Glorious Conqueror from the Shakyas, I bow down.

To the One Gone Beyond, the Great Destroyer, Destroying with Vajra Essence, I bow down.

To the One Gone Beyond, the Jewel Radiating Light, I bow down.

To the One Gone Beyond, the King with Power over the Nagas, I bow down.

To the One Gone Beyond, the Leader of the Warriors, I bow down.

To the One Gone Beyond, the Glorious Blissful One, I bow down.

To the One Gone Beyond, the Jewel Fire, I bow down.

To the One Gone Beyond, the Jewel Moonlight, I bow down.

To the One Gone Beyond, whose Pure Vision Brings Accomplishments, I bow down.

To the One Gone Beyond, the Jewel Moon, I bow down.

To the One Gone Beyond, the Stainless One, I bow down.

To the One Gone Beyond, the Glorious Giver, I bow down.

To the One Gone Beyond, the Pure One, I bow down.

To the One Gone Beyond, the Bestower of Purity, I bow down.

To the One Gone Beyond, the Celestial Waters, I bow down.

To the One Gone Beyond, the Deity of the Celestial Waters, I bow down.

To the One Gone Beyond, the Glorious Good, I bow down.

To the One Gone Beyond, the Glorious Sandalwood, I bow down.

To the One Gone Beyond, the One of Unlimited Splendour, I bow down.

To the One Gone Beyond, the Glorious Light, I bow down.

To the One Gone Beyond, the Glorious One without Sorrow, I bow down.

To the One Gone Beyond, the Son of the Desireless One, I bow down.

To the One Gone Beyond, the Glorious Flower, I bow down.

To the One Gone Beyond, who Understands Reality, Enjoying the Radiant Light of Purity, I bow down.

To the One Gone Beyond, who Understands Reality, Enjoying the Radiant Light of the Lotus, I bow down.

To the One Gone Beyond, the Glorious Gem, I bow down.

To the One Gone Beyond, the Glorious One who is Mindful, I bow down.

To the One Gone Beyond, the Glorious One whose Name is Extremely Renowned, I bow down.

To the One Gone Beyond, the King Holding the Banner of Victory over the Senses, I bow down.

To the One Gone Beyond, the Glorious One who Subdues Everything Completely, I bow down.

To the One Gone Beyond, the Victorious One in All Battles, I bow down.

To the One Gone Beyond, the Glorious One Gone Beyond to Perfect Self-control, I bow down.

To the One Gone Beyond, the Glorious one who Enhances and Illuminates Completely, I bow down.

To the One Gone Beyond, the Jewel Lotus who Subdues All, I bow down.

To the One Gone Beyond, the Foe Destroyer, the Fully Enlightened One, the King with Power over Mount Meru, always Remaining in the Jewel and the Lotus, I bow down.

All you thirty-five buddhas, and all the others, those gone beyond, foe destroyers, fully enlightened ones and transcendent destroyers who are existing, sustaining and living throughout the ten directions of sentient beings' worlds – all you buddhas, please give me your attention.

In this life, and throughout beginningless lives in all the realms of samsara, I've created, caused others to create, and rejoiced at the creation of negative karma such as misusing offerings to holy objects, misusing offerings to the sangha, stealing the possessions of the sangha of the ten directions; I have caused others to create these (negative actions) and rejoiced at their creation.

I've committed the five extreme negative actions, caused others to create them and rejoiced at their creation. I've committed the ten non-virtuous actions, involved others in them, and rejoiced in their involvement.

Being obscured by all this karma, I've created the cause for myself and other sentient beings to be reborn in the hells, as animals, as pretas, in irreligious places, amongst barbarians, as long-lived gods, with imperfect senses, holding wrong views, and being displeased with the presence of a buddha.

Now before these buddhas, transcendent destroyers who have become transcendental wisdom, who have become the compassionate eye, who have become witnesses, who have become valid and see with their omniscient minds, I am confessing and accepting all these actions as negative. I will not conceal or hide them, and from now on I'll refrain from committing these negative actions.

Buddhas and transcendent destroyers, please give me you attention: in this life and throughout beginningless lives in all the realms of samsara, whatever root of virtue I've created through even the smallest acts of charity such as giving one mouthful of food to a being born as an animal, whatever root of virtue I've created by keeping pure morality, whatever root of virtue I've created by abiding in pure conduct, whatever root of virtue I've created by fully ripening sentient beings' minds, whatever root of virtue I've created by generating bodhicitta, and whatever root of virtue I've created of the highest transcendental wisdom.

Bringing together all these merits of both myself and others, I now dedicate them to the highest of which there is no higher, to that even above the highest, to the highest of the high, to that which is higher than the foe destroyer. Thus I dedicate them completely to the highest, fully accomplished enlightenment.

Just as the buddhas and transcendent destroyers of the past have dedicated, just as the buddhas and transcendent destroyers of the future will dedicate, and just as the buddhas and transcendent destroyers of the present are dedicating, in the same way I make this dedication.

I confess all my negative karmas separately and rejoice in all merits. I implore all the buddhas to grant my request that I may realize the ultimate, sublime, highest transcendental wisdom.

To the sublime kings of human beings living now, to those of the past, and to those who have yet to appear, to all those whose knowledge is as vast as an infinite ocean, I go for refuge.

Appendix,
Glossary,
Suggested Further
Reading

1 Phonetics of Prayers in Tibetan

PRAYERS TO BE SAID AT THE START OF A MEDITATION SESSION

1 *Prayer of refuge and bodhicitta*
Sang. gyay chö.dang tsog.kyi chog.nam.la
Jang.chub bar. du dag.ni kyab. su.chi
Dag.gi jin.sog gyi.pay sö.nam.gyi
Dro.la pen.chir sang.gyay drub.par.shog (3 times)

2 *The four immeasurable thoughts*
Sem.chen tam.chay de.wa.dang de.way gyu.dang
   den.par gyur.chig
Sem.chen tam.chay dug.ngel.dang dug.ngel kyi
   gyu.dang del.war gyur.chig
Sem.chen tam.chay dug.ngel me.pay de.wa.dang
   mi.drel.war gyur.chig
Sem.chen tam.chay nye.ring chag.dang nyi.dang
   drel.way dang.nyom.la nay.par gyur.chig

3 *Refuge in the guru*
La.ma sang. gyay la.ma.chö
De.zhin la.ma ge.dün.te
Kun.gyi je.po la.ma.te
La.ma nam.la kyab.su.chi (3 times)

4 *The seven limbs*
 Go.sum gü.pay go.nay chag.tsel.lo
 Ngö.sham yi.trul chö.trin ma.lü.bül
 Tog.me nay.sag dig.tung tam.chay.shag
 Kye.pag ge.wa nam.la je.yi.rang
 Kor.wa ma.dong bar.du leg.zhug.nay
 Dro.la chö.kyi kor.lo kor.wa.dang
 Dag.zhen ge.nam jang.chub chen.por.ngo

5 *Mandala offering*
Long mandala offering
 Om vajra bhumi ah hum / Wang.chen ser.gyi sa.zhi / Om
 vajra rekhe ah hum / Chi.chag ri kor yug.gyi / kor.wä
 ü.su / ri gyäl.po ri.rab / Shar lu.pag.po / Lho
 dzam.bu.ling / Nub ba.lang.chö / Jang dra.mi.nyän /
 Lü.dang lü.pag / Nga.yab.dang nga.yab.zhän /
 Yo.dän.d'ang lam.ch'og.dro / Dra.mi / nyän.dang dra.mi /
 nyän gyi.da / Rin.po.che ri.wo / Pag.sam gy'i.shing /
 Dö.jö.ba / Ma.mö.pa.yi lo.tog / K'or.lo rin.po.che /
 Nor.bu rin.po.che / Tzün.mo rin.po.che / Lön.po
 rin.po.che / Lang.po rin.po.che / Ta.chog rin.po.che /
 Mag.pön rin.po.che / Ter ch'en.pö.yi bum pa /
 Geg.ma / Treng.wa.ma / Lu.ma / Gar.ma /
 Me.tog.ma / Dug.pö.ma / Nang.säl.ma / Dri.chab.ma /
 Nyi.ma da.wa / Rin.po.che dug / chog.lä nam.par
 gyäl.wä gyäl.tsän / Ü.su.lha.dang.mi / päl.jor pun.sum
 tsog.pa / Ma.tsang.wa me.pa / Tzang zhing yid.du
 wong.wa / Di.dag drin.chen tza.wa / Kye.per du.yang
 nye.me shak.ya / Dang gyü.par chä.pä päl.dän / La.ma
 dam.pa nam.dang / Chen.po lha.tsog kor.dang chä.pä
 nam.la / Zhing.gam ül.war.gyio / Tug.je dro.wä dön.du
 zhe.su.söl / Zhe.nä dag.sog dro.wa mar.gyur / nam.kä
 ta.dang nyam.pä sem.chän tam.chä.la / Tug.tze.wa
 chen.pö go.nä jin.gyi lab.tu.söl

Outer mandala

Sa.zhi pö.kyi jug.shing me.tog.tram
Ri.rab ling.zhi nyi.day gyen.pa.di
Sang.gyay zhing.du mig.te ül.war.gyi
Dro.kün nam.dag zhing.la chö.par.shog

Inner mandala

Dag.gi chag. dang mong.sum kye.pay.yül
Dra.nyen bar.sum lü.dang long.chö.chay
Pang.pa me.par bül.gyi leg.zhe.nay
Dug.sum rang.sar dröl.war jin.gyi.lob

Idam guru ratna mandalakam niryatayami

PRAYERS TO BE SAID AT THE CONCLUSION OF A MEDITATION SESSION

6 *Dedication of merit*

Ge.wa di.yi nyur.du.dag
La.ma sang.gyay drub.gyur.nay
Dro.wa chig.kyang ma.lü.pa
De.yi sa.la gö.par.shog

7 *Bodhicitta prayer*

Jang.chub sem.chog rin.po.che
Ma.kye pa.nam kye.gyur.chig
Kye.pa nyam.pa may.pa.yi
Gong.nay gong.du pel.war.shog

PRAYER TO TARA

Om chom.den.day.ma pag.ma dröl.ma la chag.tsel.lo
Chag.tsel dröl.ma tare pel.mo
Tuttara.yi jig.kün sel.ma
Ture dön.nam tam.chay ter.ma
Soha yi.ge che.la rab.tu

THE EIGHT MAHAYANA PRECEPTS

Preliminary prayers
Refuge in the guru
 La.ma sang.gyay la.ma.chö
 De.zhin la.ma ge.dün.te
 Kun.gyi je.po la.ma.te
 La.ma nam.la kyab.su.chi (3 times)

Generating bodhicitta
 Dag.dang zhen.dön drub.lay.du
 Dag.gi jang.chub sem.kye.do (3 times)

Purifying the environment
 Tam.chay du.ni sa.zhi.dag
 Seg.ma la.sog me.pa.dang
 Lag.til tar.nyam be.dur.yay
 Rang.zhin jam.por nay.gyur.chig

Offering prayer
 Lha.dang mi.yi chö.pay.dzay
 Ngö.su sham.dang yi.kyi.trul
 Kun.sang chö.trin la.na.may
 Nam.kay kam.kun kyab.gyur.chig

Mantra to bless and increase the offerings
 Om namo bagawatay / bendzay sarwa parma dana /
 tathagata ya / arhatay / samyak sambuddhaya / tayata / om
 bendzay bendzay / maha bendzay / maha taydza bendzay /
 maha biya bendzay / maha bodhitsita bendzay / maha
 bodhi mendo pasam damana bendzay / sarwa karma awa /
 rana bisho dana bendzay soha (3 times)

Expressing the power of truth
 Kön.chog sum.gyi den.pa.dang
 Sang.gyay dang jang.chub sem.pa tam.chay kyi
 Jin.gyi.lab dang tsog.nyi yong.su dzog.pay
 Nga.tang chen. po.dang
 Chö.kyi.ying nam.par dag.ching sam.gyi mi.kyab.pay
  tob.kyi de.shin nyi.du gyur.chig

Invocation

  Ma.lu sem.chen kun.gyi gön.gyur.ching
  Du.te pung.chay mi.zay jom.dzay.lha
  Ngö.nam ma.lu yang.dag kyen.gyur.pay
  Chom.den kor.chay nay.dir sheg.su.söl

The seven limbs and *mandala offering* (page 202)

Taking the ordination

  Chog.chu na shug. pay sang.gyay dang /
  Jang.chub.sem.pa tam.chay dag.la gong.su.söl / Ji.tar
  ngön.gyi de.zhin sheg.pa dra.chom.pa yang.dag.par
  dzog.pay sang.gyay ta.chang shay.ta.wu / Lang.po
  chen.po / Ja.wa jay.shing je.pa jay.pa / Kur.bor.wa /
  Rang.gi.dön je.su tob.pa / Si.par kun.tu jor.wa yong.su
  zay.pa / Yang.dag.pay ka / Leg.par nam.par dröl.way
  tug / Leg.par nam.par dröl.way she.rab chen de.dag.gi /
  Sem.chen tam. chay kyi dön.gyi chir.dang / Pen.par
  ja.way chir.dang / Dröl.war ja.way chir.dang / Mu.ge
  me.par ja.way chir.dang / Nay.me.par ja.way chir.dang /
  Jang.chub kyi chog.kyi chö.nam yong.su dzog.par
  ja.way chir.dang / La.na.me.pa yang.dag par dzog.pay
  jung.chub nge.par tog.par ja.way.chir so. jong
  yang.dag.par dzay.pa de.zhin.du dag.ming (say your
  name) di.zhe.gyi way.kyang / Du.di nay zung.te ji.si
  sang.nyi.ma ma.shar.gyi bar.du / Sem.chen tam.chay kyi
  dön.gyi chir.dang / Pen.par ja.way chir.dang / Dröl.war
  ja.way chir.dang / Mu.ge me.par ja.way chir.dang / Nay
  me.par ja.way chir.dang / Jang.chub kyi chog.kyi chö.nam
  yong.su dzog.par ja.way chir.dang / La.na me.pa yang.dag
  par dzog.pay jang.chub nge.par tog.par ja.way.chir so.
  jong yang.dag.par lang.war gyi.wo (3 times)

The prayer of commitment of keeping the precepts

  Deng.nay sog.chö mi.ja.zhing / Zhen.gyi nor.yang lang.
  mi. ja / Trig.pay chog.kyang mi.chö.ching / Dzun. gyi
  tsig.kyang mi.ma.o / Kyön.ni mang.po nyer. ten. pay /
  Chang.ni yong.su pang.war.ja / Tri.ten che.to

mi.ja.zhing / De.zhin du.ma yin.pay.zay / Dri.dang
treng.wa gyen.dang.ni / Gar.dang lu.sog pang.war.ja /
Ji.tar dra.chom tag.tu.ni / Sog.chö la.sog mi.je.tar /
De.zhin sog.chö la.sog.pang / La.me jang.chub
nyur.tob.shog / Dug.ngel mang.trug jig.ten.di / Si.pay
tso.lay dröl.war.shog

Mantra to purify broken precepts

Om ahmoga shila sambara bara bara maha shuda sato
payma bibu kita budza dara dara samanta ahwalokite hum
pay soha (7 or 21 times)

Dedication prayers

Trim.kyi tsul.trim kyön.me.ching
Tsul.trim nam.par dag.dang.den
Lom.sem me.pay tsul.trim.kyi
Tsul.trim pa.röl chin.dzog.shog

Jang.chub sem. chog rin.po.che
Ma.kye pa.nam kye.gyur.chig
Kye.pa nyam.pa me.pa.yi
Gong.nay gong.du pel.war.shog

Kye.wa kun.tu yang.dag la.ma.dang
Drel.me chö.kyi pel.la long.chö.ching
Sa.dang lam.gyi yön.ten rab.dzog.nay
Dor.je chang.gi go.pang nyur.tob.shog

Ge.wa di.yi kye.bo.kun
Sö.nam ye.she tsog.dzog.shing
Sö.nam ye.she le.jung.way
Dam.pa ku.nyi tob.par.shog

Jam.pel pa.wö ji.tar kyen.pa.dang
Kun.tu zang.po de.yang de.shin.te
De.dag kun.gyi je.su dag.lob.chir
Ge.wa di.dag tam.chay rab.tu.ngo

Du.sum sheg.pay gyel.wa tam.chay.kyi
Ngo.wa gang.la chog.tu ngag.pa.de

Dag.gi ge.way tsa.wa di.kun.kyang
Zang.po chö.chir rab.tu ngo.war.gyi

THE BODHISATTVA'S CONFESSION OF
MORAL DOWNFALLS

Dag.ming (say your name) di.zhe gyi.wa / Du.tag.tu
la.ma.la kyab.su.chi.wo / Sang.gyay la kyab.su.chi.wo /
Chö.la kyab.sy.chi.wo / Ge.dün la kyab.su.chi.wo /
Tön.pa chom.den.day de.zhin sheg.pa dra.chom.pa
　　yang.dag.par dzog.pay sang.gyay pel.gyel.wa shak.ya
　　tub.pa.la chag.tsel.lo /
De.zhin sheg.pa dor.je nying.pö rab.tu jom.pa.la
　　chag.tsel.lo /
De.zhin sheg.pa rin.chen ö.tö.la chag.tsel.lo /
De.zhin sheg.pa lu.wang gi gyel.po.la chag.tsel.lo /
De.zhin sheg.pa pa.wö de.la chag.tsel.lo /
De.zhin sheg.pa pel.gye.la chag.tsel.lo /
De.zhin sheg.pa rin.chen me.la chag.tsel.lo /
De.zhin sheg.pa rin.chen da.ö.la chag.tsel.lo /
De.zhin sheg.pa tong.wa dön.yö.la chag.tsel.lo /
De.zhin sheg.pa rin.chen da.wa.la chag.tsel.lo /
De.zhin sheg.pa dri.ma me.pa.la chag.tsel.lo /
De.zhin sheg.pa pel.jin.la chag.tsel.lo /
De.zhin sheg.pa tsang.pa.la chag.tsel.lo /
De.zhin sheg.pa tsang.pay jin.la chag.tsel.lo /
De.zhin sheg.pa chu.lha.la chag.tsel.lo /
De.zhin sheg.pa chu.lhay lha.la chag.tsel.lo /
De.zhin sheg.pa pel.zang.la chag.tsel.lo /
De.zhin sheg.pa tzen.den pel.la chag.tsel.lo /
De.zhin sheg.pa zi.ji ta.yay.la chag.tsel.lo /
De.zhin sheg.pa ö.pel.la chag.tsel.lo /
De.zhin sheg.pa nya.ngen me.pay pel.la chag. tsel.lo /
De.zhin sheg.pa se.me kyı.bu.la chag.tsel.lo /
De.zhin sheg.pa me.tog pel.la chag.tsel.lo /
De.zhin sheg.pa tsang.pay ö.zer nam.par röl.pay
　　ngön.par kyen.pa.la chag.tsel.lo /
De.zhin sheg.pa pay. may ö.zer nam.par röl.pay

ngön.par kyen.pa.la chag.tsel.lo /
De.zhin sheg.pa nor.pel.la chag.tsel.lo /
De.zhin sheg.pa dren.pay pel.la chag.tsel.lo /
De.zhin sheg.pa tsen.pel shin.tu yong.dag.la chag.tsel.lo /
De.zhin sheg.pa wang.pö tog.gi gyel.tsen gyi
    gyel.po.la chag.tsel.lo /
De.zhin sheg.pa shin.tu nam.par nön.pay pel.la
    chag.tsel.lo /
De.zhin sheg.pa yul.lay shin.tu nam.par gyel.wa.la
    chag.tsel.lo /
De.zhin sheg.pa nam.par nön.pay sheg.pay pel.la
    chag.tsel.lo /
De.zhin sheg.pa kün.nay nang.wa kö.pay pel.la
    chag.tsel.lo /
De.zhin sheg.pa rin.chen pay.may nam.par nön.pa.la
    chag.tsel.lo /
De.zhin sheg.pa dra.chom.pa yang.dag.par dzog.pay
    sang.gyay rin.po.che dang pay.ma.la rab.tu zhug.pa
    ri.wang.gi gyel.po.la chag.tsel.lo /
De.dag la sog.pa chog.chü jig.ten.gyi.kam tam.chay na
    de.zhin sheg.pa dra. chom.pa yang.dag.par dzog.pay
    sang.gyay chom.den.day gang ji.nye.chig zhug.te
    tso.zhing zhe.pay sang.gyay chom.den.day de.dag
    tam.chay dag.la gong.su.söl /
Dag.gi kye.wa di dang / Kye.wa tog.may ta.ma
    ma.chi.pa nay kor.wa na kor.way kye.nay tam.chay du
    dig.pay.lay gyi.pa.dang / Gyi.du tsel.wa.dang /
    Gyi.pa.la je.su yi.rang.wa.am / Chö.ten gyi kor.ram /
    Ge.dun gyi kor.ram / Chog.chu ge.dun.gyi kor trog.pa
    dang / Trog.tu chug. pa dang / Trog.pa.la je.su yi.rang
    wa.am / Tsam ma.chi.pa ngay.lay gyi.pa dang / Gyi.du
    tzel.wa dang / Gyi.pa.la je.su yi.rang wa.am /
    Mi.ge.wa chu.lay kyi.lam yang.dag par lang.wa.la
    zhug.pa dang / Jug.tu tzel.wa dang / Jug.pa.la je.su
    yi.rang wa.aṃ / Lay. kyi drib.pa gang.gi ḍrib.nay dag
    sem.chen nyel.war chi wa.am / Du.drö kye.nay.su chi
    wa.am / Yi.dag kyi yul.du chi wa.am / Yul ta.kob
    tu.kye wa.am / La.lor kye wa.am / Lha.tse ring.po

nam.su kye wa.am / Wang.po ma.tsang.war gyur
wa.am / Ta.wa log.par dzin.par gyur wa.am /
Sang.gyay jung.wa.la nye.par mi. gyi.par gyur.way
lay.kyi drib.wa gang.lag.pa de.dag tam.chay
sang.gyay chom.den.day ye.she.su gyur.pa / Chen.du
gyur.pa / Pang.du gyur.pa / Tsä.mar gyur.pa /
Kyen.pay zig.pa de.dag.gi chen.ngar töl.lo / Chag.so /
mi.chab.wo / Mi.be.do / Län.chay kyang chö.ching
dom.par gyi lag.so / Sang.gyay chom.de.day de.dag
tam.chay dag.la gong.su söl / dag.gi kye.wa.di dang /
Kye.wa tog.may ta.ma ma.chi.pa nay kor.wa.na
kor.way kye.nay zhen.dag.tu jin.pa ta.na du.drö kye
nay.su kye.pa.la zay.kam chig.tzam tzel.way ge.way
tza.wa gang lap.pa.dang / Dag.gi tsul.trim sung.way
ge.way tza.wa gang lag.pa.dang / Dag.gi tsang.par
chö.pay ge. way tza.wa gang lag.pa dang / Dag.gi
sem.chen yong.su min.par gyi.pay ge.way tza.wa gang
lag.pa dang / Dag.gi jang.chub chog.tu sem.kye.pay
ge.way tza.wa gang lag.pa dang / Dag.gi la.na me.pay
ye.she.kyi ge.way tza.wa gang lag.pa de.dag tam.chay
chig.tu du.shing dum.te dom.nay la.na ma.chi.pa dang /
Gong.na ma.chi.pa dang / Gong.may yang gong.ma /
La.may yang la.mar yong.su ngo.way la.na me.pa
yang.dag.par dzog.pay jang.chub.tu yong.su ngo.war
gyi.wo / Ji.tar day.pay sang.gyay chom.den.day
nam.kyi yong.su ngö.wa dang / Ji.tar ma.jön.pay sang
gyay chom.den. day nam.kyi yong.su ngo.war.
gyur.wa dang / Ji.tar da.tar zhug.pay sang.gyay
chom.den.day nam.kyi yong.su ngo.war dzay.pay
de.zhin.du dag.gi kyang yong.su ngo.war gyi.wo /

　　Dig.pa tam.chay ni so.sor shag.so sö.nam tam.chay
la.ni je.su yi.rang.ngo / Sang.gyay tam.chay la.ni
kul.zhing söl.wa deb.so / Dag.gi la.na me.pay ye.she
kyi chog.dam.pa tob.par gyur.chig /
Mi.chog gyel.wa gang.dag da.tar zhug.pa dang /
Gang.dag day.pa dag.dang de.zhin gang.ma.jön /
Yön.ten ngag.pa ta.yay gya. tso da.kun.la / Tel.mo
jar.war gyi.te kyab.su nye.war chi.wo

Glossary

arya noble one; a superior being having attained bare perception of the true nature of reality

asura a celestial being who enjoys greater comfort and pleasure than human beings, but who is nevertheless dissatisfied and suffers from jealousy

bhagawan epithet of a buddha, meaning one who has destroyed all obstacles, who is endowed with realizations and who has transcended the world

bodhicitta the aspiration to attain full enlightenment in order to enlighten all beings

bodhisattva a being who is striving for enlightenment with the motivation of bodhicitta, i.e. in order to free all other beings from confusion and suffering

buddha an awakened one; a fully enlightened being; one who has overcome all obstacles and completed all good qualities and is therefore able to benefit all other beings to the maximum extent

buddahood see *enlightenment*

cause and effect the process whereby virtuous actions lead to happiness and non-virtuous ones to suffering; the law of karma *central channel* the principal channel of the psychic nervous system, in which the mind travels throughout the body; it runs from the crown of the head to the tip of the sexual organ, parallel to the spine

compassion the wish that all beings be separated from their problems

cyclic existence the cycle of death and rebirth, fraught with suffering and dissatisfaction, that arises from ignorance of the true nature of reality

delusion an aspect of the mind that misunderstands the nature of things and deals with people and situations in a mistaken, harmful way, thus resulting in problems and pain. Examples are anger, pride and jealousy

dharma spiritual teachings; any technique or knowledge that frees us from confusion and suffering

emptiness the actual way in which all things exist, the absence of the apparent inherent existence of things

enlightenment complete elimination of all negative aspects of the mind and perfection of all positive qualities

foe destroyer (Sanskrit, *arhat*) one who has attained nirvana, or complete liberation from suffering, but has not yet attained enlightenment

graduated path teachings outlining the progressive training of the mind leading to enlightenment

guru (Tibetan, *lama*) spiritual teacher and guide

hungry spirit (Sanskrit, *preta*) a non-human being who experiences intense suffering of hunger, thirst, heat and cold

ignorance the root of cyclic existence; not knowing the way things actually exist

inherent existence the falsely conceived mode of existence of things; something's apparent existence from its own side, independent of parts, causes or the process of conceptual imputation; that which is negated by emptiness

Je Tzong Khapa great 14th century Tibetan scholar, teacher and yogi

karma see *cause and effect*

lama see *guru*

liberation the state of complete personal freedom from suffering and its causes (delusion and karma)

love the wish that all beings be happy

Mahayana great vehicle of those seeking enlightenment for the sake of benefitting others

Maitreya the next founder-buddha to come, once Shakyamuni Buddha's teachings have disappeared from the world

mandala practice of mentally offering the entire universe; a special environment

mantra words of power; syllables, usually Sanskirt, recited during certain meditational practices

meditation the process of becoming deeply acquainted with one's own mind

meditational deity a visualized figure, used in meditation, representing a specific aspect of the fully enlightened mind; for example, Tara and Avalokiteshvara

merit insight, power or energy bestowed on the mind when one performs virtuous actions

Mount Meru the centre of the universe according to Buddhist cosmology

nirvana see *liberation*

one gone beyond, one thus gone (Sanskrit, *tathagata*) epithet of a buddha

pure land a state of existence outside samsara where all conditions are favourable for becoming fully enlightened; buddha field

refuge the attitude of relying upon someone or something for guidance and help; in Buddhism one takes refuge in the three sublime ones: buddha, dharma and sangha

renunciation the attitude of complete detachment from the experiences of samsara, seeing that there is no true pleasure or satisfaction to be found within it

samsara see *cyclic existence*

sangha monastic community following the teachings of Buddha; more specifically, the assembly or arya beings on the path to liberation and enlightenment; spiritual friends who help us in our practice of dharma *sentient being* a being who has not yet reached enlightenment

Shakyamuni the founder-buddha of the present age

sura celestial being who enjoys the highest pleasures to be found in cyclic existence

tantra advanced teachings of the Buddha leading to the speedy attainment of enlightenment; Mantrayana; Vajrayana

tathagata see *one gone beyond*

three jewels, three sublime ones the objects of Buddhist refuge: buddha, dharma and sangha

vajra (Tibetan, *dorje*) diamond-sceptre held by certain meditational deities that represents bodhicitta, the mind of enlightenment; adamantine, pure

Vajrayana the path of tantra

Suggested Further Reading

Awakening the Mind
Basic Buddhist Meditations

Geshe Namgyal Wangchen

Based on the teachings of the Tibetan saint Tsong Khapa, these techniques help replace depression, anger, and other forms of mental pain with tranquility, compassion, and wisdom. The methods of meditation presented here have helped people overcome their problems for centuries.

"...replete with excellent guidance on Mahayana practice."—*The Tibet Journal*

272 pages, 0-86171-102-5, $14.95

Transforming Problems into Happiness

Lama Zopa Rinpoche

Commenting on a nineteenth-century Tibetan text of instructions and practical advice for everyday spiritual living, Lama Zopa Rinpoche literally teaches us to be happy when we are not by bringing about the changes in attitude that permit us to live a happy and relaxed life in which external circumstances no longer rule us.

"A masterfully brief statement of Buddhist teachings on the nature of humanity and human suffering." —*Utne Reader*

104 pages, 0-86171-194-7, $12.95

Being Nobody, Going Nowhere
Meditations on the Buddhist Path

Ayya Khema

"Few introductory books are both simple and profound. Ayya Khema has achieved both…"—North American Board for East-West Dialogue

"Of special help are the Ayya's simple, grounded instructions to aid us in our everyday lives to develop calmness of mind and insight into our human existence…forthright and resolute guidance for the journey."
—*Karuna: A Journal of Buddhist Meditation*

192 pages, 0-86171-052-5, $14.95

Introduction to Tantra

Lama Thubten Yeshe

What is tantra? Who is qualified to practice it? How should it be practiced? What are the results? According to Buddhism, every human being has the potential to achieve profound and lasting happiness. And according to the tantric teachings of Buddhism, this remarkable transformation can be realized very quickly if we utilize all aspects of our human energy—especially the energy of our desires.

"No one has summarized the essence of tantra as well as Thubten Yeshe does here." —*Religious Studies Review*

176 pages, 0-86171-021-5, $15.95

Advice from a Spiritual Friend

Geshe Rabten & Geshe Dhargey

Based on practical Buddhist verses of thought transformation from centuries ago, this profound wisdom reaches out to people from all walks of life. No matter what your spiritual orientation, you will benefit from this sage advice.

"Reading this book is akin to taking a personal retreat with two kindly and wise teachers."—*NAPRA ReVIEW*

160 pages, 0-86171-193-9, $15.95

Mindfulness in Plain English

Henepola Gunaratana

This step-by-step guide to Insight Meditation is truly practical and direct. Venerable Gunaratana's conversational style and use of everyday examples imbue the basic teachings of Vipassana meditation with unsurpassable clarity and wit.

"...of great value to newcomers...especially people without access to a teacher."—Larry Rosenberg, author of *Breath by Breath*

"A masterpiece. I cannot recommend it highly enough." —Jon Kabat-Zinn, author of *Wherever You Go, There You Are*

208 pages, 0-86171-064-9, $14.95

Only a Great Rain

A Guide to Chinese Buddhist Meditation

Master Hsing Yun

Modern meditation master Hsing Yun brings to life the vast legacy of Chinese Buddhist meditative practices in straightforward and engaging language.

"There is useful stuff in this book for all who are interested in cultivating their meditation practice." —*Tricycle*

160 pages, 0-86171-148-3, $14.95

Be an Island

The Buddhist Practice of Inner Peace

Ayya Khema

"In disarmingly practical language, Ayya Khema teaches us that true practice is getting the tiny details of life right, the middling moments—thinking before we speak, recognizing greed and generosity in ourselves and others, making the mind pliable at all times. This is the type of book you'll want to go back to, placing it near an altar or spiritual nook for easy access." —Religion Editor, Amazon.com

160 pages, 0-86171-147-5, $14.95

Journey to the Center
A Meditation Workbook

Matthew Flickstein

Whether your goal is to reduce stress or to gain mastery over your inner life, this simple, straightforward guidebook is the tool to use for learning why and how to meditate. Using a unique workbook format, Matt Flickstein teaches you how to gain mental clarity and remove obstacles, and helps you to identify the appropriate insights for each stage of your journey to spiritual and psychological maturity.

224 pages, 0-86171-141-6, $15.95

Wisdom Energy
Basic Buddhist Teachings

Lama Yeshe and Lama Zopa Rinpoche

"This is a superb book....presents basic Buddhist teachings with great lucidity and clarity."—*Resource*

"...immensely practical advice and suggestions."—*The Middle Way Journal of Buddhist Studies*

160 pages, 0-86171-170-X, $14.95

Tibetan Buddhism from the Ground Up
A Practical Approach for Modern Life

B. Alan Wallace

Here at last is an organized overview of the teachings of Tibetan Buddhism, beginning with the basic themes of the sutras—the general discourses of the Buddha—and continuing through the esoteric concepts and advanced practices of tantra. This accessible, enjoyable work doesn't stop with theory and history but relates timeless spiritual principles to the pressing issues of modern life, both in terms of our daily experience and our uniquely Western world view.

"A happy find for anyone seeking to incorporate Buddhist principles into spiritual practice."—*NAPRA ReVIEW*

228 pages, 0-86171-075-4, $15.95

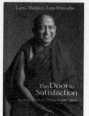

The Door to Satisfaction

The Heart Advice
of a Tibetan Buddhist Master

Lama Zopa Rinpoche

Lama Zopa reveals the essential meaning of an ancient thought-training text that he discovered in his retreat cave high in the Himalayas of Nepal. The message is simple: you can stop all problems forever and gain perfect peace of mind by practicing the thought-training methods explained herein. Open this book and open the door to a timeless path leading to wisdom and joy.

184 pages, 0-86171-058-4, $12.50

The Fine Arts of Relaxation, Concentration and Meditation

Ancient Skills for Modern Minds

Joel & Michelle Levey

"By far the best plain-language, down-to-earth, practical, easy-to-read book on mental training." —*Mind-Body Wellness*

"...a thoroughly useful, practical guidebook offering a distillation of many years of study and practice." —*Yoga and Health*

232 pages, 0-86171-040-1, $14.95

Landscapes of Wonder

Discovering Buddhist Dhamma
in the World Around Us

Bhikkhu Nyanasobhano

In eighteen inspiring essays, Bhikkhu Nyanasobhano communicates the essence of Buddhism. His examination appeals to both practitioners and those interested in broadening their knowledge of Buddhism through an enjoyable literary exploration.

"...one of the most melodious new voices in Buddhism."—Amazon.com

192 pages, 0-86171-142-4, $14.95

The Meaning of Life
From a Buddhist Perspective
His Holiness the Dalai Lama

The Dalai Lama presents the basic worldview of Buddhism while answering some of life's most profound and challenging questions. He bases his explanation on the twelve links of dependent-arising as depicted in the famous Buddhist image of the wheel of life.

"...studded with jewels...pointing out how to bring together the theory of the Buddhist teachings and the practice of ordinary life."—*Shambhala Sun*

164 pages, 0-86171-173-4, $15.95

The World of Tibetan Buddhism
An Overview of Its Philosophy and Practice
His Holiness the Dalai Lama

"...the definitive book on Tibetan Buddhism by the world's ultimate authority."—*The Reader's Review*

"...the Dalai Lama explains in brief but lucid detail every aspect of the Tibetan path to enlightenment."—*Body, Mind, Spirit*

224 pages, 0-86171-097-5, $15.95

The Good Heart
A Buddhist Perspective on the Teachings of Jesus
His Holiness the Dalai Lama

The Dalai Lama provides an extraordinary Buddhist perspective on the teachings of Jesus, commenting on well-known passages from the four Christian Gospels including the Sermon on the Mount, the parable of the mustard seed, the Resurrection, and others.

"Sparkling wit and compassionate understanding mark these penetrating insights of the Dalai Lama into spiritual foundations of two of the world's great religious traditions. Highly recommended." —*Library Journal*

224 pages, 0-86171-138-6, $14.95